GOVERNMENT SOCIAL SURVEY

Handbook
for
Interviewers

by Jean Atkinson

A manual for Government Social Survey
interviewing staff, describing practise and
procedures on structured interviewing.

LONDON
HER MAJESTY'S STATIONERY OFFICE
1968

Foreword

This is a manual for Government Social Survey interviewing staff, describing practice and procedures on structured interviewing. It is being placed on public sale as a result of the growing interest in field work techniques amongst market research workers, local government and universities both here and abroad.

GOVERNMENT SOCIAL SURVEY
JANUARY 1969

SBN 11 700028 0

Index

Index

Chapter 1

THE WORK AND PURPOSE OF THE GOVERNMENT SOCIAL SURVEY

The Government Social Survey became a Government Department in April 1967. This marked the completion of twenty-six years as a research unit working on behalf of many parts of the Government: from an initial role of dealing with war-time problems up to the present time when we continue to carry out numerous studies on matters of social and economic interest.

Throughout its history the Government Social Survey has aimed to help public departments deal with public issues by using the method of sample survey enquiries to make direct contact with individual members of the public in order to obtain representative information about their circumstances, conditions or opinions. It is part of the network of public research organisations and statistics divisions which help to provide the information on which public policy is shaped, and which helps to evaluate the progress made in developing public services to meet the needs of the population. But whereas most other Government enquiries are addressed to organisations, such as business firms or institutions, the Government Social Survey's work is concerned with individual members of the public. It therefore acts as a bridge between the Government and the population, making it possible for the Government to keep in touch with the circumstances and opinions of the general public.

During more than a quarter of a century the Government Social Survey has worked on very many public issues in nearly every field of social and economic research except that of political opinion. The studies which it carries out are nearly all asked for by Government Departments or Royal Commissions but the methods used are devised by the staff of the Survey. Most Government Social Survey reports consist of material which is collected by the interviewing staff who are, therefore, the indispensable foundation for its work.

3

In what ways has the Survey been able to help the Government? The Government Social Survey makes a continuing contribution to public statistics. For example, the continuing Family Expenditure Survey is used to show how people's spending habits change over time and in this way it enables the Ministry of Labour to keep the official Cost of Living Index up to date. The same survey shows how earnings and income received from public sources varies from year to year amongst different sections of the population.

The Government Social Survey has also at various times organised continuing surveys of the various forms of transport used and of the incidence of illness and disability amongst all parts of the population. Such surveys are organised on a very large scale.

Most Government Social Survey studies, however, are not continuous but are made to throw light on a particular problem facing the Government or to help with the work of a Royal Commission or a public Committee set up to advise the Government. Surveys of housing conditions, of the way a Rent Act works, of the steps which need to be taken to find the staff for children's homes, or of the circumstances under which old people live and the steps taken to help them, are examples of work done by us on social issues. In the economic field surveys have been made of labour mobility, that is to say how people move from job to job and place to place; and many studies have been made related to the ways in which technical information can be conveyed to those who ought to be using the most up-to-date methods.

Much survey work is concerned with the study of opinions and attitudes. For example, the work done for the Royal Commission on the Police to show how the public and police feel about their mutual relationships; or the study devised to show how aircraft noise round London (Heathrow) Airport affects the local population; or what work circumstances and motives people have in deciding when they will take holidays.

In all these ways the Government Social Survey provides information about people's conditions and how they feel about them thus providing a realistic foundation on which Government Departments can base a particular course of action or on which they can assess the effects of a projected policy.

4

THE METHODS AND CONDITIONS OF WORK

The methods used in all these studies are very varied. In most cases interviewing is the basic method and information is obtained by asking people a carefully drawn up and tested list of questions. Sometimes, as in budgetary enquiries or nutritional studies, people are asked to keep a record of the way they spend their money over a short period of time, or of the weights of different foodstuffs eaten during a week. Sometimes the Government Social Survey draws material from existing files and subjects it to a process of analysis from which the answers to particular problems can be found. In some studies, such as those related to road safety or the work done by nurses in hospitals, the information required is obtained by observation of actual behaviour under conditions of everyday life and work.

In general the Government Social Survey bases its report on information obtained from a **sample only** of all people concerned and all the material available. In the development of research methods and especially in the use of sampling techniques the Government Social Survey is regarded as one of the most technically advanced organisations in the world, and many independent research organisations come to us for technical assistance with the design of their own enquiries.

Since the Government Social Survey has to meet the needs of all Government Departments and the range of problems it works on is correspondingly wide, a wide range of techniques and methods has to be used; and indeed the Government Social Survey has continued to help Government Departments over such a long period of time because its methods and techniques have been adapted to the changing needs of Departments. It is this wide range of available methods and extensive experience of different forms of research which has made it possible also for the Survey to help independent bodies and universities from time to time.

Present-day society gets more and more complex. At the same time public responsibility for ensuring adequate standards of economic efficiency and social welfare has become much wider than in earlier times. Public bodies which, under our parliamentary system, are charged with these responsibilities need direct, representative and factual information about the way people live and their attitudes, opinions or their conditions and circumstances if they are to do their work efficiently. The Government Social Survey exists and organises its activities in order to make a substantial contribution to these purposes.

Chapter 2

THE ROLE OF FIELD BRANCH OF THE GOVERNMENT SOCIAL SURVEY

In the Government Social Survey we want to establish and maintain the most direct contact between the source of research, namely the research officer and yourself as the person who collects the information.

For this reason we have no regional offices. However, in an organisation of our size it is not practical for you to work directly to the research officer. He is engaged on an individual study which may last a year or more from start to finish, during which time only one month may consist of field work. There are many research officers, each of whom will require the interviewers' services at some time in the year. What we have in the Government Social Survey is a certain number of Headquarters staff who concentrate on methods of interviewing, and the recruitment, training and field supervision of interviewers. Colloquially we are called the "Field Branch" and your contact with research staff is mainly through us.

Field Branch's task is to realise the aims of any piece of research for our research staff, by providing interviewers to collect data for them and by using our amassed specialist knowledge to advise on the best means of collecting data.

A research officer needs to know that there are interviewers:

(a) available whenever he wants field work carried out.

(b) ready trained on approach, in gaining co-operation from all kinds of people and versed in the discipline of collecting data in a uniform and predictable way. (This is essential when some 150 interviewers are working on a study.)

We therefore:

(a) **Provide trained field staff**

    (i)   recruit interviewers.

    (ii)   give initial training in structured interviewing technique.

    (iii)   help develop interviewers' skill in this technique and others and test performance from time to time.

    (i) (ii) & (iii)
        are carried out so that we have sufficient inter-viewers with the right skills available for each survey.

(b) **Programme field work**

    (iv)   dovetail field work on different surveys so as to provide a continuous field programme, taking into account survey priorities, the number of trained interviewers available each month and the size of the sample on each survey.

(c) **Manage work in progress**

    (v)   invite interviewers to work on each study.

    (vi)   organise a series of briefings for them.

    (vii) prepare and despatch all documents to interviewers, and in turn book in interviewers' work and keep account of response rate and quality of work.

    (viii) handle interviewers' queries on work in progress and supervise the actual field work.

(d) **Act as Personnel Branch for interviewers**

    (ix)   keep records of interviewers' history of work, their training, availability and aptitudes. In turn we advise them on any aspect of interviewing technique.

(e) **Provide an advisory service for research staff**

    (x)   use skilled interviewers and staff to advise on question construction, schedule layout and ways of presenting projects to the public.

    (xi)   work with research staff on devising new inter-viewing methods or develop alternative ways of handling new subject matter as it occurs.

    (x) & (xi)
        are done by experiment on pilot and pre-pilot stages of surveys.

(f) **Undertake methodological study**

Study the effect on the results of different ways of data collection as opportunities occur for this on work in pro-gress. Look out for possible interviewer effect on results.

Chapter 3

SYSTEM OF SUPERVISION AND TRAINING OF
INTERVIEWERS

Interviewing is a highly specialised job and structured interviewing even more so. In fact many people do not take easily
to the work. In our training we emphasise that it is for the
recruit to decide, along with us, whether or not she is suited
to the work. She needs to have an aptitude for it, to be in
sympathy with our function and methods and to acquire skill in
a reasonably short time.

All recruits who are invited to begin training with the Government Social Survey are told that their training will follow in
stages. At the end of each stage an assessment is made of their
progress before they are allowed to proceed to the next stage.

STAGES

1 3-day Initial Office Training Class

Each interviewer recruit is sent this Handbook to study and
invited to attend an office training session, which lasts three
days. During this course the basic method of interview (as
outlined in the Handbook) is dealt with by means of lecture,
discussion and recruit participation on "dummy", or practice
interviewing. Prior study of the Handbook is essential to get
the most out of the course. At the end of the three days we
decide whether or not to offer field training.

2 First Field Training

This is given on actual field work and takes place as soon as
possible after attendance at the office course. A field training
officer accompanies you in the field. She will give a demon-
stration interview and stay with you and observe your first few
interviews. She teaches you the practical application of what
has been discussed during the office training session. You need
to make full use of this individual tuition period and learn from
the constructive criticism which the trainer can offer you. You
must discuss and clarify with her any uncertainties about interviewing so that you are sure what to do by the time you are left
alone.

3 Probationary Service

Although stages 1 and 2 constitute basic training, clearly, as in any job, once you know the fundamentals there is much more to learn about working efficiently and achieving extra skill. We therefore consider your work on at least the first three quotas to be, in a sense, probationary. We reckon that after this amount of practice you should have overcome any beginner's faults and be capable of interviewing people with ease. This will only be the case if you think about your performance at each interview, enquire of us how to improve it and eliminate any difficulties you are meeting. It is probable that in the course of your probationary field work some further field supervision will be given. The same or another training officer will join you to watch your interviews on your 2nd or 3rd quota. She may demonstrate her interviewing to you again. She will want to see you carry out several interviews before she suggests ways in which to improve your interviewing technique.

4 End of Probation Test

You are invited to the office for a test at the end of the probationary period. You are asked to complete a written paper questioning your knowledge and understanding of the survey principles as laid down in the Handbook. You are asked to carry out several trial interviews on a test schedule, which will have been sent to you earlier for study. The informants are office staff unversed in interviewing technique. We tape-record your interviews and later mark them for accuracy in method of questioning and recording. Your score in this test is then considered in conjunction with field training officers' reports on your progress during probationary field work. In turn we take into account your field availability and the efficiency and economy with which you have completed field work allocated to you during this period. Anyone not achieving a reasonable overall standard of work at this stage would be told that we could not keep her name on our panel of interviewers. To all people who have passed probation satisfactorily a report is sent giving details of the test performance. We comment on all aspects of your work in order to show what to concentrate on in the future.

Continuous/Broken service and re-engagement of Interviewers

Any interviewer who cannot undertake field work for at least six months is temporarily resigned and given field supervision on the first survey she undertakes on re-employment. If the break in service is longer than this and/or an interviewer was relatively inexperienced before departure, we would expect her to attend another initial Training Class and to serve a further period of probationary service on her return to work.

5 Training and supervision after probationary service

(a) *Field*

No interviewer will reach her potential unless she is constantly
critical of her own work. You need to keep in touch with us,
raise queries, take advice offered and read more about interviewing methods from books which we can suggest to you.

Field supervision of field work. Subsequent to passing the
test you will be observed at work in the field at irregular intervals.
This means you must be prepared for someone to join you at any
time, on any quota. Normally you will hear from training staff
by telephone or letter to the effect they want to join you on your
next day's work. Whilst we do not want you to change your
routine of work drastically in order to have something to show
a staff member, it is helpful if you can meet her wishes and
work on the days when she can come to your area. Remember,
we have a large field force. Training staff try to see as many
interviewers as possible per month; their own timetables are,
if anything, more complex than an interviewer's with her informants. These visits are meant to be helpful both to you and
us. We can only vouch for the accuracy and uniformity of our
work if we know what standard of field performance is being
achieved on each survey. And for you it is important to have
someone with whom to discuss interviewing methods from time
to time.

Training staff invariably join you whenever we know the
survey is of a somewhat different nature from any you have
undertaken before. For example, on your first record-keeping
study, such as the Family Expenditure Survey, you would be
accompanied and given guidance on approaching whole households. If ever you are given a survey where the subject matter,
type of questioning or method of contact worries you in some
way, if we have not said you are to be accompanied, do tell us
if you want advice. It is no admission of failure to do this.
We would far rather help you (and this may be done very easily)
than have you go out lacking confidence in a survey, because
error or lack of response might be the result in such a case.
In a sense your work is assessed annually by us and we try to
let you have a note on your progress in the year and the standard
of work you have achieved. Whereas we hope that our experienced
interviewers will work for us for many years, it has to be
remembered that accuracy and precise performance of duties
are expected of you throughout. If at any time we find your
work unsatisfactory then we must withdraw our offer of work
at once.

(b) *Office (returns of work)*

Your work on each survey is checked as it comes into the office.
We note delays and the number of schedules which it is found
to be necessary to return to you. Sometimes the work sent
in results in our accompanying you on the rest of the quota, or
we decide to call back on some of your informants to see what
their reactions were to your visit. These recalls are not meant
as a check on whether you visited the house in the first place.
You are all persons chosen for your integrity, conscientiousness
and interest in our work. When we make recalls on the public
we advise you of the particularly good or not so good aspects
of your work which we have noted. Incidentally, we expect
that the schedule we had back from you, relating to the household on which we are recalling, will already give us notes on
any odd circumstances of the interview; any broken appointments, any questions omitted in error, so that whatever detail
we check will be a verification of what we already know.

(c) *Further formal training*

You will be given the chance to attend further office training
groups as your skill in interviewing develops. On later visits
to the office certain aspects of interviewing are considered
more fully. We might discuss probing, matters of approach
to the public and piloting technique. Whenever possible some
of you will go into Coding Branch to see what happens to the
interviews you return and what problems are created by lack
of information from the interviewer on what took place during
the interview.

(d) *Briefings*

You will attend the office for briefing on each of the surveys
on which you work. Part of the briefing is meant to deal again
with basic interviewing method. Once the current survey material
has been explained at the briefing we practise on the new schedule in large, or preferably small, groups with the research
officer present. Field personnel are also there to advise and
comment on your technique of handling various types of question.
These briefings give you the opportunity of observing how interviewers other than yourself tackle questions. You do need to
remember that no one is demonstrating a 'perfect' interview
to you when they are participating in briefings. You may have
to accept (after discussion, if necessary) that some of what you
have seen is an example of what not to do just as much of what

to do. Generally we arrange for someone from Field Branch to be in the briefing room the half-hours before and after the briefing session in order to answer your individual queries. These may relate to things you have encountered during the last month's field work. Even though the survey to which you refer is then finished it does not invalidate your queries if they are about principles of interviewing which you will need to apply on forthcoming work.

Participate fully in briefings, querying anything on which you are in doubt, whether the purpose of the survey, the meaning of certain questions or the way in which you are meant to handle any of them. Our aim in so thoroughly preparing you for your field task is to ensure that by the time field work starts you will be fully conversant with the enquiry. During the briefing, when the research officer gives a fuller description of the purpose and background to the survey, take notes on what is being said. From this material you can then decide on various ways of explaining the survey to the public.

Normally briefings last from 10 a.m. to 5 p.m. and you must be able to stay the whole day. For some surveys a day and a half is required. In the case of the Family Expenditure Survey we allow two days, again expecting you to remain up to 5 p.m.

At briefings **any** points that are not clear from the schedule and instructions should be queried with the research or field training staff. We try to organise several briefings per study so that no one meeting is so overcrowded that your own personal difficulties cannot be communicated.

Chapter 4

STAGES IN PRODUCTION OF A SURVEY

	(Stage)	(Activities)
1.	REQUEST	SURVEY MOOTED by Government or other public body. COST FACTOR DECIDED. REQUEST made for TREASURY AUTHORITY to undertake survey.
2.	RESEARCH INTO PROBLEM	RESEARCH OFFICER put in charge of survey. He produces a proposed DRAFT SCHEME FOR SURVEY. He consults: SAMPLING: Sample type, source and size discussed. FIELD: Undertake pilot (trial) stages from free to semi to structured interviewing. CODING: Analyse pilot material. Research officer, sampling, field and coding DISCUSS PILOT FINDINGS; DECIDE FORMAT for main stage of survey. PREPARATION of address lists, schedules. Dates of work in each branch agreed.
3.	MAIN STAGE	FIELD: Brief interviewers, field survey on agreed structured schedule. CODING: Precheck schedules. Categorise all responses. COMPUTING: Produce tables relating all responses.
4.	CON-CLUSION	RESEARCH OFFICER: Writes report, or provides data in table form for client to combine with other material.

Field work is one part of the whole process of carrying out a survey, and all parts of the process are interdependent. It is important for you to realise that much thought, skill, research and specialist experience goes into each survey on which you work.

If you look again at the make-up of a survey you will see that once we have decided on the interview as our means of data collection the research officer's thinking is geared to the problems of collecting information in the face-to-face situation. All the careful coding and tabulating of responses is based on the assumption that the material that has been collected in the field is the material we set out to collect.

1 The request

On receiving a request for a survey it is decided whether or not the problem is suited to enquiry by survey methods. It could be that required information exists within another Government Department or as a piece of independent research. The survey is accepted if data does not exist elsewhere and we know how to contact the relevant population. The best means of collecting the information is then considered: if it is something readily observable then we would use interviewers as observers, for instance to know how people behave at an exhibition, or to measure space on an office accommodation survey, or to measure height of blind people's walking sticks (all of which we have done in the past). Often one cannot observe but must question to elicit facts and attitudes held on social matters. Since it is cheaper to send a letter rather than an interviewer if the survey is on a simple subject we use a postal questionnaire.

However, projects put to us are mostly complex, requiring masses of answers on subjects which could not readily be explained, and on which one could not hope to achieve a good response from a letter contact. **A complex structured interview is the one in which we specialise,** although we do employ other techniques as surveys warrant them.

Once a decision is reached on the suitability of a project it is costed on our experience of interviewing similar populations on similar subjects. The commissioning department (our client) then seeks authority for the survey from Treasury; they put their case for needing such a study and state the estimated cost. Not all surveys are approved and any that are authorised are clearly of considerable importance to the Government.

2 Research into problem

Individual research officers tend to specialise in particular fields of study, for example, in Education, Health or Delinquency. The Director chooses which research officer will be responsible for a study on the basis of that particular officer's interest and previous experience in similar fields. The research officer has to know the clients' problem before he can advise and in turn reach agreement with them on the type of information to be collected. This is an intensely active stage for the research officer, who must read much on his subject and take into account past work in the same field before deciding the form his enquiry will take.

Specialist (technical) branches of the Government Social Survey are brought into the picture by the researcher. Sampling, Field, Coding and Computing Branches in turn are told what may be required of them and asked to contribute their specialist knowledge to the preparation of the survey. The contribution of each specialist branch is mentioned below in the order in which it is usually consulted. On any one study this order may change; on one survey sampling will present major problems whilst on another it will be field work.

Sampling Branch decide, with the research officer, whether the information is to be collected from a random sample of the total population or from special groups, such as elderly people or adolescents. Which population is relevant depends on the nature of the problem and the kind of information sought. The sampling officer takes part in preliminary discussions with the commissioning department in order to know more about the scope of the survey. In turn the nature of the analyses is relevant to the sampling officer since the size of the sample set depends, to some extent, on how detailed the analyses will be. A sample needs to be big enough to provide enough data on as many small cells (sub-sections of the population) in which the department may be interested.

Field Branch's Pilot Role

The amount and type of pilot or trial work to be carried out before we field a main survey is dependent on the aims of the study and the amount of previous research into the subject that has been undertaken within the Government Social Survey or by other researchers.

From group discussions and free interviews, undertaken by interviewers, the research officer can see the scope of a subject and in turn advise the client on general lines of enquiry to pursue. Much depends on the clarity of the research officer's brief: if there is a prescribed area of enquiry, which has already been researched in part by us or others, then the research officer will produce a semi-structured schedule of questions at once for field trial.

15

On a pilot survey our task is to determine:

(i) **The public's reaction to the subject of the survey**.

(ii) To consider **ways of putting the subject over to the public to achieve high response.**

(iii) **The best order in which to introduce topics,** i.e. from least personal; covering general aspects of the enquiry first and proceeding to more complex issues.

(iv) **Ways in which to word questions to elicit precise data.** This involves determining the function of questions, whether to collect facts or opinions and whether to do this by open or closed questioning.

(v) **Whether the object of the survey justifies the complexity of the questions** we want to ask. We are wholly dependent on the goodwill of the public and cannot subject them to unnecessary or painful questioning.

(vi) **The length of time the public can be expected to give for an interview,** in view of the level of interest endemic in the subject.

(vii) **The best layout of schedules** (questionnaires) so as to make them manageable in the most difficult field conditions.

Experienced interviewers work on pilots. The kind of instruction they have on the type of interview undertaken is not covered in great detail in this Handbook but elsewhere.

Field Branch's contribution at the pilot stage of a survey is considerable. We look at both the quantity and quality of response, judging whether the research officer's words had the right effect on the public and suggesting to him words with greater impetus.

Words or phrases in common usage come from interviewers; advice on the public resistance or antipathy to questions and constructive thought on how to overcome it; comments on the length of interview and the most reliable sequence for the questioning all have to be thrashed out.

Coding Branch analyse pilot findings and comment on the quantifiability of material.

From the pilot our aim is to produce a set of questions which can be used for the main stage of the survey, without alteration, in many thousands of interviews. We want questions which are understood by informants, willingly answered by them and taken by the whole population unambiguously to mean the same things.

All technical branches co-operate in the production of the final schedule for a survey. The Field depend on Sampling for address lists; Coding depend on interviewers to return schedules for analysis; and the level of efficiency and accuracy at which Coding, Computing, and interviewers, can work, depends on the facility with which the schedule is laid out.

3 Main Stage of Field Work

When the final schedule is produced, the research officer provides instructions which amplify the questions and set out the
way in which the survey is to be handled. These instructions
are specific because it is important that each interview is conducted in the same way if we are to take as comparable the data
produced by many interviewers. Interviewers are always
allowed time in which to study the instructions and to do practice
or dummy interviews before beginning work on the survey.
Particular instructions for the survey are meant to be carried
out to the last detail. For most surveys much of the schedule
is handled as on other studies and basic ways of questioning
are not explained per survey but in the other chapters of this
Handbook.

Answers given to interviewers have to be sorted by Coding
Branch and counted by the Computing Branch. The work of
these two branches is described below.

The Work of Coding Branch

When the completed questionnaires have been returned to H.Q.
they are sent to the Coding Branch for the stage of processing
known as primary analysis, or, more commonly, coding. The
coding function can be briefly described as the translation of
written answers on schedules into symbols that are suitable for
mechanical processing.

A brief description of all the stages of the work of Coding
Branch follows:

(a) The pre-checking or editing of schedules

Before the actual coding process can begin it is necessary
for two basic conditions to be satisfied. These are:

(i)   that the questions on the schedule are producing the
      kinds of answer needed by the research officer for
      a meaningful and accurate report, and

(ii) that any inconsistencies or misunderstandings on the
      part of interviewers about any of the questions are
      picked up at an early stage of the enquiry.

The process that ensures that these conditions are fulfilled
is called "pre-checking" or "editing". To do this, as soon as
completed schedules arrive in Coding Branch they are scrutinised
in detail for any omissions or inconsistencies. When misunderstandings occur the schedules are usually returned with notes
either asking for clarification or asking the interviewer to recall.

(b) Checking whole or part-pre-coded questions

There are basically three ways of recording answers to questions
on schedules. One of these is the wholly pre-coded type of
answer where the range of answers are shown as specific groups,
each of which has been given numbers or symbols to identify it
on the schedule and which the interviewer has to ring according
to an informant's responses. Another is the "open" recording
where there are no specific groups at all and the interviewer
has to write down the informant's responses in full. The third
way of recording is a combination of the two; that is where
there are a number of specific groups with numbers or symbols
to identify them which the interviewer has to ring and another
category (usually called "Others specify") which does not fit
into these specific groups where the interviewer has to record
all the answers verbatim.

In respect of answers that are pre-coded, or partly pre-coded,
these are always checked for completion or consistency. For
example, by examining the written answers to the "Other specify"
category of a partly pre-coded question, it is possible to determine how accurately the pre-coded categories have been used,
and, whether they are working correctly. Another way of checking
pre-coded information is by comparing pre-coded answers with
information from other questions on the schedule and with the
classification section. A simple illustration of how inconsistencies can be picked up would be where a person whose age has
been given as 5 yrs. was pre-coded as "working full time". In
most cases obvious inconsistencies can be corrected by this
cross-checking of information, but this is not always possible.

(c) The classification and coding of questions which are not pre-coded

For all the questions which are not pre-coded Coding Branch
has to do two things. First, the coding supervisor for that
particular survey has to devise for each question appropriate
groups or categories into which the great majority of answers
fall. (It is not, of course, possible to fit all the answers into
specific categories and for these a special "miscellaneous"
category is provided.) Secondly, the coders have to fit all the
answers from that question into these specific categories.

(i) Devising a coding frame

The term coding frame is normally used in the Government Social Survey to describe the range of categories
derived from answers to questions on the schedules which
are not pre-coded, and the method of constructing one of
these frames is as follows. First a random selection of
all answers to a particular question is listed verbatim,
this usually amounts to about 10% of the sample but it can
vary according to the size of the particular survey. These
answers are then carefully examined by the coding super-

18

visor who devises the different categories into which the answers fall. Ideally, all categories should be mutually exclusive but, in some cases, particularly with attitude or opinion questions, it is sometimes difficult to do this. After consultation with the research officer the categories are then given a coding symbol or number. Coding frames usually consist of up to 12 categories, but in some cases are very much larger depending on the nature of the question.

A simple illustration of the way answers are grouped is shown by the following example of a coding frame taken from an actual survey. Informants who had had more than one paid job were asked the question:

"Why did you leave your last job?"

The answers fell into the following categories and were given numerical symbols as follows:

Low Wages................. 1

Lack of security........... 2

Holidays not long enough..... 3

Working hours too long...... 4

No prospect of promotion.... 5

Made redundant 6

Unhealthy working conditions. 7

Wanted a change of work 8

Other answers (specify below) 9

....

The importance of adequate probing and the necessity for interviewers not to economise in the use of words when recording can best be demonstrated by an answer which was, when probed, recorded as

"We don't get enough time off. (Exp.) We only get a fortnight's holiday a year."

If this had been recorded merely as

"We don't get enough time off",

it would have resulted in the loss of meaningful information as coders would not have been able to tell whether it meant

"Holidays not long enough" - code 3,

or

"Working hours too long" - code 4.

(ii) The coding of the answers.

The next process is the actual coding operation itself.
This is done by the coding supervisor giving each coder
in his team the responsibility for coding every answer to
a question, or a block of related questions, on all the
schedules of a particular survey, until all answers have
been coded. All coding operations are then checked.
Coders have to work at considerable speed and in this
context the importance of clear, legible handwriting and
the obtaining of unambiguous information cannot be over-
emphasised. It is also important to use only officially
sanctioned abbreviations as obviously any others will not
necessarily be understood by coders.

After all the coding operations have been completed the
schedules are then passed to Computing Branch for the machine
and tabulating process.

The work of Computing Branch

Punching

When the schedules are sent to the punch section all the answers
given by the informants have been given code numbers. It is
the job of the punch section to translate these code numbers into
holes punched in a card. The sort of card used by the Government Social Survey is about 4" × 8" in size and is divided into
80 sections, called columns. In any one of the columns it is
possible to punch out any twelve holes which are called from top
to bottom Y, X, O, 1, 2, 3, 4, 5, 6, 7, 8, 9.

Before the cards for a survey are punched, a card design is
made. This design allots to each question the number of columns,
called a field, necessary to contain the answers, e.g. sex will be
given one column but age would have two – one for tens of years
and one for the units. To contain all the answers on most
schedules it is necessary to have more than one card. Each
card will then have its own design.

By punching the cards to a fixed design, all cards punched on
that survey contain the answers to a particular question in the
same column on each card and the particular answer to that
question is given by the hole in that column.

After the cards are punched they are checked by a verifier
who, in effect, repeats the whole process again. Any discre-
pancies between what has been punched by the operator and the
verifier operator are eliminated.

Machining

When the cards have been punched and verified, the answers
given by informants are accurately indicated by the positions of
the holes in the cards. Machines can rapidly sort out and count
the cards to provide the tables which go to make up the report.

Machines vary in complexity and each type has its own
particular purpose. However, the object of them all is to translate the holes in the cards, and therefore the informants' answers,
into figures. Present machining speeds vary from 6,000 to
12,000 cards per hour. This variation in speed is due to the
degree of complexity in relating the information punched in the
various fields to effect the analysis required by the research
officer. This analysis usually takes the form of tables showing
the relationship between two kinds of information, e.g. the way
in which age varies with the amount of annual income.

If there is sufficient volume of analysis to be carried out on
the data, or a complex analysis is required, the information on
the punched cards is transferred on to magnetic tape, making a
tape recording which can then be read and processed by computers working at very fast speeds.

Editing

The tables from the machines are then headed to show to which
information the figures relate.

Next the tables are checked. First of all to see if they are
self-consistent, e.g. if every informant is asked a particular
question then the total of all answers must equal the number of
informants, and secondly to see that they check with previous
tables, e.g. the number of persons in each income group must
be the same on every table where income group appears.

The next stage will vary from survey to survey and will depend
upon what the research officer hopes to discover from the tables.
One of the two main steps follows. If the table deals with numbers
of replies, the table will be percentaged to show the proportion
of the sample giving each answer. If the table deals with quantity,
e.g. the amount of expenditure on certain goods, the table will
be averaged to show the average expenditure by different groups
of the population.

In addition to this, various statistical tests may be made on
the tables which help the research officer to evaluate the data,
and, to help others understand them, some tables may be shown
in diagrammatic form.

The work of the Computing Branch comes to an end when the
figures appearing in the written report are checked against the
original tables.

4 Report Writing

The research officer will have been actively involved in all the foregoing stages of his survey. He has the responsibility of writing up the results and explaining the decisions he made on the form the interviewing took and the way the data was coded and analysed. The report does not consist merely of the presentation of facts, except in those few cases where the client department has asked only for statistical material as a source of information for themselves. Mostly the research officer must, beside presenting the facts, attempt to show what they mean; how they are related to one another, and what general conclusions can be drawn from them.

Not all clients have sufficient knowledge of the sort of material a survey produces to interpret it fully for themselves; and many people are too busy to attempt it. It is the responsibility of the research officer to carry out this interpretation on behalf of the general reader of the report. He therefore tries to work out a theory, or hypothesis, which will account as fully as possible for the material he has in front of him. The final stage in writing is then the presentation of any general conclusions which may have emerged from the main body of the report. In this stage all the conclusions from the earlier branches are gathered together. These conclusions are usually embodied in a brief summary which sets out the main findings of the survey, and which forms an introduction to the whole report.

Reports are often published as White Papers and as such are available to anyone interested in the subject matter: economists, statisticans, sociologists would all make use of our surveys. The reports are the property of the commissioning department. Not all reports are available for general circulation since some studies are designed to help the client on an organisational or internal problem such as recruitment to one of the Services or police force.

Sometimes research officers produce additional findings which are of methodological interest and these are then published by our own department.

Chapter 5

SAMPLING

1 Introduction

We should all be familiar with the censuses of population, which
take place in this country every ten years, when every household in the country is visited and information is obtained about
the household and its occupants. From the data collected,
reports are prepared showing the number of dwellings and the
sizes of households occupying them, the age and sex distribution
of the population and other basic figures.

For day-to-day operational purposes and the making of
policy decisions by Departments and Commissions, censuses
would take too long, be too costly and altogether too unwieldy an
operation to serve as a practical method of collecting information.

In a great many instances the only practical way of relatively
quickly obtaining information about the general population or any
special group of population is by means of a well-designed and
skilfully conducted SAMPLE SURVEY. By a sample survey we
mean that instead of approaching the whole of any population and
asking appropriate questions we take only some of the relevant
population in such a way that those we take are a representative
"sample" of the whole.

A survey can be designed so that it represents adequately
almost any population or some specialised section of population;
more detailed information can be collected by it than on a
census because the data are being collected by highly trained
staff, usually in an interview situation; in turn the data can be
processed more quickly because there is not the same bulk as
with a census, so that the results are made available as near
as possible to the time the survey was fielded, at a time when
they are most relevant.

2 A Random Sample

You can take a sample of almost anything. Samples are taken
in factories to help control quality; in the home you take a sip
of tea or coffee or taste a little of your cake mixture before
baking to see if it is satisfactory. This you do once it has been
thoroughly stirred, or mixed. In other words, you take a
sample and if that "taste" is as it should be then you conclude
that all is satisfactory with the tea, cake or product of the
factory. You are saying that your sample is representative of
the whole. So it is with a sample survey: provided the sample
is properly selected from the whole of the relevant population
so that it is representative in all respects, then conclusions
can be drawn from the information obtained from the sample
which will equally well apply to the whole population from which
the sample was taken.

In the case of a sample survey it means that we have to have some way of drawing a sample from the whole of the particular population. We need to have access to some records which list everyone within the relevant population.

Having such a list we would then take one person in every so many and, providing we did not set out deliberately to include particular names but counted every one **once,** then we would have a representative sample. The names picked would have come up by chance and no one person is any more likely to have been picked than any other. The inference is that each one selected is representative of all others like him in the population and therefore the different types of people there are would appear in the sample in the same proportions as they did in the population from which the sample was drawn. If the population contained 50% males and 50% females then the sample could be expected to contain the same proportions.

Technically, a sample which is drawn by chance in this way is known as a "random" or "probability" sample. However, it is random only in a statistical sense, i.e. EVERY MEMBER OF THE RELEVANT POPULATION HAS BEEN INCLUDED AND EVERYONE HAS HAD THE SAME CHANCE OF BEING PICKED.

Sample Size

In addition to the sample being representative, it must also be of a size which will permit detailed analysis of the data collected.

No two members of the population are going to be identical in all respects. Therefore in taking a sample of the population each selected person represents a number of others like him in many respects but not absolutely identical to him. Consequently estimates made from the data collected from any sample are liable to a certain margin of error simply because it is a sample, but provided random sampling methods have been used this sampling error can be calculated. In general (all other things being equal), the larger the sample the smaller the error.

From any survey, data are required about sub-sections of the population as well as for the population as a whole, e.g. results obtained from a sample of the general population would probably need to be analysed separately for males and females, in five-or ten-year age groups, in different income groups and by other factors relevant to the subject of the survey. The sample must, therefore, be large enough for data obtained from the smallest of these groups to be given with a degree of accuracy which is statistically defensible. Since size of a sample affects the cost of a survey our task is to determine the minimum sized sample to take on any study which will yet achieve our purposes.

Size is determined mainly as a result of consultation between research officer, client department and Sampling Branch. In Government Social Survey samples of certain population may be as low as a few hundred. Frequently, sample size is between 1,000 and 5,000 and there are occasions when it needs to rise to 20,000 or more.

Source of a Sample

At the onset of a survey it has to be decided what population has to be sampled and how this can best be done. For the purposes of random sampling there has to be a "frame" from which the sample units can be selected. Such a "frame" may exist, e.g. in the form of a list, or lists of individuals, addresses, offices or works which go to make up that population, or it may be necessary to compile a suitable one. Every member of the specific population must be included in the frame, and included once only otherwise not everyone has the same chance of selection, in which case the sample could no longer be said to be representative.

For general population surveys the frame we use is most likely to be the Electoral Register, or the Rating (sometimes called Valuation) Lists.

The Electoral Register lists **persons** eligible to vote at elections, namely persons aged 21 years and over, together with the addresses at which they lived at the time the Electoral Register was last drawn up (it is revised annually).

The Rating (or Valuation) Lists give all the separately rated units, i.e. "**dwelling** units" in this country. but not necessarily the names of the persons who live within the dwelling units.

These two registers are the most comprehensive lists available in this country from which to draw a sample of people or dwellings. Both have minor deficiencies but these are known to us. In reports we state the source of our sample and thereby indicate any peculiarities or shortcomings that we knew to exist in the basic design of our sample.

Some surveys require samples of particular populations, e.g. doctors, police, school teachers or undergraduates, and then we have to seek out some list which contains every doctor in the country or all policemen; the same criteria apply to any such records used as a frame, namely that every member of the population must be included once only in our draw.

25

SAMPLED UNIT

A NAMED INDIVIDUALS If we want to know the attitudes of the public on a given issue, or factual data related to the individual's way of life, we sample **named persons.**

Such a sample can be one of individuals within the general population or within special populations (teenagers, elderly persons). On such a sample YOU INTERVIEW THE PERSON NAMED AND NO OTHER. Since we seek the opinions of the adult population of Great Britain the Electoral Register is the "frame" from which samples are often drawn. Each individual named in the register is counted once and so has a chance of coming up in our sample.

B ADDRESSES On studies such as Family Expenditure or Housing Costs it is relevant to use a sample where the unit selected consists of a group of people. For such a sample we ignore the names in a register and count only the **addresses.**

YOU INTERVIEW THE PERSON or PERSONS (according to instructions) WHO LIVE AT THE GIVEN ADDRESS AT THE TIME WHEN YOU GET THERE.

When **addresses** have been sampled you may be required to see

(i)   all the persons living at that address

(ii)   only a specific member of each household who fills a particular role, such as "housewife" or "head of household".
You will have to know your instructions for that survey to ensure you interview only the right person(s) (as at (i) or (ii)).

For surveys requiring a sample of households we have to take either a sample of addresses from the Electoral Register or of rateable units from the Rating Lists.

Note, to help you check that you have the right address, you may be given the name(s) of the occupier(s) as given in the records, but you might find that these people had moved away. This does not matter. If it is a "household" survey, where you know it was the address that was sampled, you take the households living at that precise address when you get there.

Addresses sometimes accommodate more than one group of people (or catering unit), ideally the latter is what we want but, since no list identifies "households" in this way we contact such groups by starting from a list of addresses.

Where addresses contain more than one household (our term for a group of people living together, being catered for by the same person) we refer to such addresses as multi-household addresses. The proportion of these in a sample is comparatively small, though concentrated, in certain conurbations such as London.

There are special instructions on handling multi-households at the address. In some surveys you may be asked to list all households and then select a sample of them according to set instructions for that individual survey.

3 Special populations

In some cases from an address list sample our aim is to establish:

(iii) a special population e.g. adolescents or elderly persons. There are no complete lists of these groups of people (e.g. a list of pensioners would not be a complete list of elderly). When we require to obtain a sample of a section of the population in this way there is no means of knowing beforehand at which addresses such people live. You have to carry out a further stage of sampling for us by calling at all the addresses in the sample and establishing for us which households contain eligible persons and which do not.

It is as important for us to know the latter as the former because in analysing the results of a survey and referring back to the sample drawn and achieved we check the accuracy of our sample against census data. For this reason any time you are asked to sort out which addresses contain eligible persons (according to certain criteria for the survey) it is most important that you establish eligibility accurately by seeing in person people who live at each given address. The percentage we report as ineligibles must be verified as such so that our figures on ineligibles never mask any persons who really were eligible but who could not co-operate for some reason.

From time to time we need to draw samples from sources for which records are not kept centrally, e.g. Education Surveys for which we may wish to select pupils from school registers. You may be asked to draw this sample for us, by going to the school armed with precise written instructions from Sampling Branch on the sampling fraction and which registers you are to use. If called on to do this the utmost accuracy is required in following the instructions and copying names chosen from the records.

Whatever the type of sample, once on field work if the given names and addresses are unidentifiable **never** take an interview until you have contacted Sampling Branch and asked for further verification of the sampled unit.

27

Method of drawing a sample

The mechanics of drawing a sample are much more complex than might have been suggested by the earlier part of this chapter. They will be described here so that you have an understanding of the length to which we go to achieve accuracy when collecting data.

Theoretically the simplest way of selecting a representative sample of, say, persons aged 21 and over in Great Britain would be to take a list of all people aged 21 and over in the country, such as the Electoral Register, and take the names at a constant interval throughout. Such a method would be impractical for an interview survey. For example, for a sample of 3,000 adult individuals it would mean taking about every 10,000th name throughout the register. The people would be very thinly scattered over the whole country and the time and cost of an interviewer travelling from one member of the sample to another would make such a procedure completely uneconomic. We want a representative sample of the population and the only way of obtaining it is to take a random sample: at the same time we want to avoid each interviewer having a very widespread sample address list.

Fortunately it is possible to fulfill the vital condition for a representative sample, namely, that every member of the population under study should have an equal chance of being selected, in a more practical way. This can be done by carrying out "multi-stage sampling". In other words, instead of selecting people throughout the whole of a single list for Great Britain we can select a "random" sample of "primary" units or areas and then draw a random sample from the lists of people within these selected primary units. In a two-stage sample design we can first select a sample of areas in which people live and then, within the selected areas only, select from all people shown on the lists covering those areas.

The first stage therefore in designing a multi-stage national sample is to select a representative sample of areas. Various types of area are used as "primary" units; frequently they are local authority areas, i.e. boroughs, urban districts and rural districts; sometimes smaller units such as wards and parishes are used and sometimes counties or combinations of local authority areas are the units. However, the same general principles of selection apply whatever the unit used.

Selecting a Sample of Areas

The people of this country live in local authority areas of which there are approximately 1, 500 in England and Wales and 430 in Scotland. These vary in type and location, and to ensure that the sample will be a representative one we divide the areas into a number of groups.

The first grouping would normally be a geographic one into the 10 standard regions into which the country is divided for statistical purposes. By grouping areas in this way we can be sure that the sample of areas is correctly distributed geographically throughout the country. These regions are the Northern, North Western, Yorkshire and Humberside, East Midlands, West Midlands, East Anglia, South Eastern, South Western, Wales and Scotland. Wales would be further subdivided into North and South-East, and Scotland into Northern, East Central, West Central and Southern. Thus we would have 14 groups of areas.

Within each of these areas we would consider how many "urban" areas (which include the boroughs and urban districts), and how many "rural" areas occur.

So far we have ensured that we would have the correct geographical spread and the right proportion of "urban" and "rural" units, but frequently it is necessary to break down these groups still further. How they should be divided will depend on the survey. Urban areas, in particular, vary considerably in population size, and some rural areas are much more densely populated than others. Some areas are highly industrialised and others are not; some urban areas are part of a large mass of urban areas known as "conurbations". Any or all of the foregoing may be used as factors by which to further re-group areas within a region.

Another factor by which areas differ and which is of importance in many of our surveys is the "economic status" of an area. Some areas may be looked upon as relatively wealthy areas and others as relatively poor and so we would use some other factor to break down our groups into even smaller groups. There is no direct means of measuring the "economic status" of an area, but one useful measure is the proportion of the total rateable value of an area as expressed by the rateable value of the dwelling accommodation in that area.

The aim in all grouping or "stratification" as it is called is to put into each group units which are most alike. Having grouped areas in this way we can then draw our random sample of areas, knowing that we shall have a sample of areas which do represent the characteristics of all areas within the country.

When we come to the stage of drawing names or addresses within the areas the operation is carried out objectively by using "Tables of Random Numbers" to begin our selection and by going through the complete list and drawing out a name/address at a regular interval from this random start, according to the instruction of the sampling officer.

STAGES IN DRAWING A NATIONAL SAMPLE

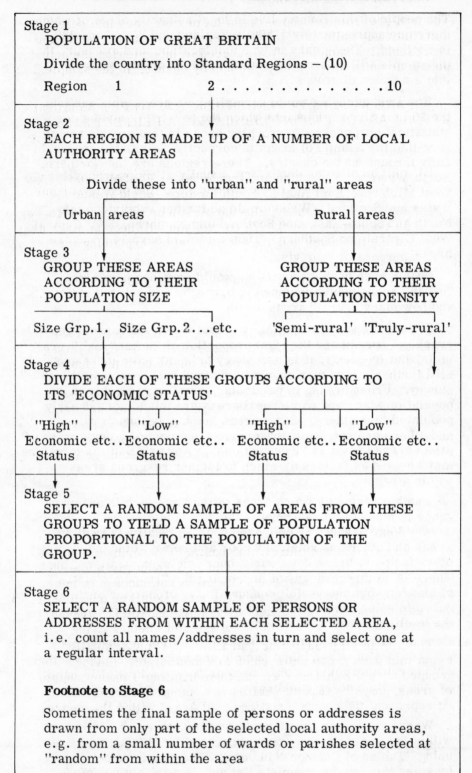

Stage 1

POPULATION OF GREAT BRITAIN

Divide the country into Standard Regions – (10)

Region   1   2 10

Stage 2

EACH REGION IS MADE UP OF A NUMBER OF LOCAL AUTHORITY AREAS

Divide these into "urban" and "rural" areas

Urban areas   Rural areas

Stage 3

GROUP THESE AREAS ACCORDING TO THEIR POPULATION SIZE

GROUP THESE AREAS ACCORDING TO THEIR POPULATION DENSITY

Size Grp.1. Size Grp.2...etc.   'Semi-rural' 'Truly-rural'

Stage 4

DIVIDE EACH OF THESE GROUPS ACCORDING TO ITS 'ECONOMIC STATUS'

"High"   "Low"   "High"   "Low"
Economic etc..Economic etc..   Economic etc..Economic etc..
Status   Status   Status   Status

Stage 5

SELECT A RANDOM SAMPLE OF AREAS FROM THESE GROUPS TO YIELD A SAMPLE OF POPULATION PROPORTIONAL TO THE POPULATION OF THE GROUP.

Stage 6

SELECT A RANDOM SAMPLE OF PERSONS OR ADDRESSES FROM WITHIN EACH SELECTED AREA, i.e. count all names/addresses in turn and select one at a regular interval.

Footnote to Stage 6

Sometimes the final sample of persons or addresses is drawn from only part of the selected local authority areas, e.g. from a small number of wards or parishes selected at "random" from within the area

Interviewer role as sampler

You will see from the above that a lot of care goes into selecting a statistically valid sample. It will only prove a defensible and representative sample, if you succeed in interviewing the actual people or units which have come up, by chance, in the sample.

WE ARE WHOLLY DEPENDENT ON YOU TO PUT AS MUCH EFFORT AS YOU CAN INTO ACHIEVING A PERFECT SAMPLE.

You will have to:

(i) call as often as necessary, usually at times inconvenient to you, frequently in the evenings, to find people at home.

(ii) take care to identify fully the person or address (whichever is the sampled unit). To do this you will need to make use of the full name and/or address before explaining the purpose of your visit.

(iii) persuade into participation as many as possible of the persons selected for interview.

The way in which a sample is drawn, up to the point at which it is sent to you to be realised, is described in detail in this chapter so that you can impress on the public both the chance by which they came to be selected for interview, as well as the scientific way in which this is done, which makes it necessary for you to gain their co-operation; when people come up in this fashion we get an accurate cross-section of the population providing the chance selection is adhered to. No person down the road whom they regard as more typical can be taken, or it would bias data.

Data on non-respondents

In our reports the sampling frame has to be described; together with the size of the sample drawn and an account given for everyone within the sample set. If you do not succeed in interviewing someone you must give us as much detail as possible of the reasons why you failed and tell us anything you know about the person missed; his approximate age and whether living alone or with other persons. This information helps us check the accuracy of our original sample and helps determine whether any unavoidable non-response does or does not invalidate data for any section of the community.

Chapter 6

APPROACH TO EMPLOY WITH THE PUBLIC

A *INITIAL CONTACT* between Interviewer and Informant

The success of the work of the Government Social Survey depends
on the goodwill of the general public; on their willingness to
co-operate in surveys voluntarily. **No one is compelled to give
an interview.** The quality of the information we obtain from the
public depends very much on how well you, the interviewer,
have explained the purpose of the enquiry and the kind of atmosphere you have managed to create between yourself and the informant during the interview.

The person we wish to interview is unlikely to have prior
knowledge of our organisation, or the survey in hand. In turn,
you are a stranger to the informant. From this unpromising
beginning it follows that you must work quickly to establish
contact with the stranger if he is to be made to feel at ease in
your company and willing to voice to you his true opinions or to
confide facts relating to his pattern of living.

Necessary Introductory Points

Before beginning to interview an informant, there are some seven points to be made to him:

(i)   **the name of our organisation.**

(ii)   **the name of the department on whose behalf the survey is being undertaken.**

(iii)   **an explanation of how he, the named person came to be selected for interview.**

(iv)   **the purpose of the survey in terms of the reasons we have been given by the commissioning department.**

(v)   **the confidential nature of the enquiry.** The confidence of those who give us information is respected under all circumstances; the identity of informants is not disclosed to anyone outside the Government Social Survey, not to another Government Department, nor to members of the public, nor to the press. In particular, reports and other analyses based on information supplied by members of the public are presented in such a way that the identity of our informants is not revealed.

(vi)   **an indication that co-operation is voluntary** though this does not necessitate the use of the actual word on every doorstep. The point is covered by asking the informant either *"May I ask you"/or, "Would you be willing to help us"/or, "Will you take part in the survey?"*

(vii)   **some indication of the length of the interview.** Never mislead people into thinking it will take a few minutes if you know it will take half or one hour. For long interviews it is sensible to quote the average time taken but indicate it could take longer if the person were particularly interested in the subject.

      In turn, you must show your informant your authorisation card, usually on entering the house. This gives weight to points (i), (v) and (vi) above.

All the above points must be covered before you begin to question a person, but the order in which you make the points and the stage at which they should be mentioned is left to your discretion, bearing in mind the following.

33

The majority of our surveys are directed at individuals or families resident in Great Britain in their capacity as private citizens, though we may be concentrating a study on a particular population such as school children, the working population or the elderly. As the people we select for interview are approached in their role as private citizens, most often we wish to contact them in their homes.

Unless instructed to do so you must not write or telephone for an appointment with your informant. **Initial contact is to be made by you in person.**

People are not usually forewarned of your visit and it is your job to **identify** the person chosen and to explain the purpose of your visit in a way that will make sense to the chosen person(s).

In calling at an address you will find the demeanour of the person you meet will help you decide how best to put the survey to them. You can judge from their facial expression where one argument is failing and a different line of appeal is necessary.

There are two stages to the initial contact at an address:

Stage 1 we will refer to as the doorstep contact (read below)

Stage 2 is what happens when you get inside the house (read page 41 onwards).

A *STAGE 1 OF CONTACT*. DOORSTEP CONTACT

KEEP YOUR DOORSTEP INTRODUCTION BRIEF. If the chosen person is immediately co-operative but shows no sign of asking you into the house, this may be because he has been interviewed by other callers who took only ten minutes. After establishing that a person can give sufficient time at that point, it is in no way impolite to suggest *"May I come inside?"*. It is conducive to a good interview to have your informant at ease inside his own home. If you have had occasion to make point (vii) above, then usually people will invite you in straightaway unless you have called at a busy time. It would be tactically correct to withdraw as soon as you realise the time is inopportune. If you try to persuade the informant to give an interview at what is a wrong time for him, you are asking for a refusal.

Similarly, if a person is full of self-doubt, or in a bad mood and consequently disinclined to co-operate when you are discussing the purpose of your call and you fear he is on the point of saying no, it sometimes helps to give oneself the chance of returning on another day.

34

Some people profess to be busy but you may judge them to be evasive. To these people you must give a careful explanation of the value to us of their participation. With this minority of the population if you sense that to press for co-operation there and then will result in them taking fright and saying no, then leave saying, *"If I may, I would like to call again some other day to see if you are then less busy"*. Providing they do not forbid you to recall at the house the chances are you will gain co-operation on recall. People appreciate the importance you attach to the interview if you do bother to come back, also on another day their mood may be happier making them more receptive to the interview.

Some people's immediate reaction is to tell you they are not typical, they do not know anything about the subject and they genuinely feel that they would be of no use to us. It is your job to explain to them that providing they were the persons whose names came up by chance for interview, then they are the only persons you wish to see. No others can replace them. You can assure them that you know they will be able to help us in the way we wish, if only they will let you talk to them. They do not have to be any sort of expert on any subject to help you.

ISSUES OF IDENTIFICATION

You need to identify the person to be interviewed before you can put over the purpose of your visit. **Correct identification is vital.** It is worth discussing here the general procedure for contacting informants because the impression you make on the would-be informant, or his family, on first sight can make or mar one's chances of gaining co-operation.

There are five observations to be made about types of sample (see chapter 5 on Sampling).

Types of sample to be identified:
  (a) Named individual.
  (b) Family "role" members.
  (c) Special age or "type" person within the population.
  (d) Whole households.
  (e) Other "special" populations.

In order to illustrate correct procedure there follow examples of approach on each type of sample.

(a) Method of Approach when Identifying an Individual

If we are concerned to know the public's attitudes on an issue then the type of sample drawn will usually consist of individuals. You will have been given a list of persons, both their christian or first names as well as surnames. Therefore your first task on reaching a house, having knocked at the door, is to identify the selected person by using his full name, the name which will be supplied to you from the electoral roll. If he or she is not at home, then indicate to whoever has come to the door that you are looking for the named person and ask at what time he or she might be in.

It is most important to try to get through to the person who has been selected for interview and to give your explanation of the reason for the visit to that chosen person.

(This chosen person will be referred to as your "informant" throughout the rest of this Handbook.)

If it transpires that you are talking to a near relative, for example wife or mother, then you may feel it advisable to produce your authorisation card and give a minimal explanation of your presence by saying, *"I am calling on behalf of the Government Social Survey, having been asked to see your (husband/son). If I may come back at the time (or night) when you say he will be in, I can explain the purpose of my visit. It is not connected with anything that he knows about, and I would like the chance to explain it to him in person".*

Our experience of trying to explain surveys secondhand suggests that to do so lessens one's chances of co-operation. Garbled versions of the reason for your visit get through to the person concerned if they come from another member of the family. It is important that, whilst refraining from going into details of the purpose of your call, you in no way create the impression that you are holding back information. It is no help to create suspicion within the mind of one of your would-be informant's relations since to do so would only hinder your chances of co-operation from the named person.

The whole essence of contacting people in person to get information is based on the knowledge that the person-to-person situation affords you the chance of summing up the informant and providing an explanation of the object of your visit in terms that he will understand. Another member of his family may differ from the named person and the kind of explanation you have given them, as to the reason for the survey, may, in fact, not appeal in any way to your informant. Or it might be that your explanation is perfectly adequate but that the intermediary is not sympathetic towards the aims of the survey, becomes prejudiced, and stops you getting through to see your chosen person.

Sometimes a named individual is available on first call, but not for interview because he is viewing you with timidity, or else incomprehension. Your chance of success rests with finding out whether anyone else lives at the address (such as husband, or daughter) so that you can come back and explain the purpose of your visit in the other person's presence. This is not to say you want to interview any but the named individual, but if someone normally relies on his relative's judgment as to the rightness of an action, you will do best in such a case to win the support of the relative in the other's presence and so establish through him real contact with your informant.

Similarly if a would-be informant says he is willing to co-operate but his spouse or other relative does not believe in surveys, and can you interview quickly before the relative gets home, do not do this. If you sense or are told of family opposition in this way, suggest calling back to see the member of the family in person, to discuss our work, so your subsequent interview is by approval. We do not want to cause any family discord.

(b) Method of Approach when Identifying a "Role" Member within a Family

On surveys aimed at collecting data on the expenditure of a group of people living together as one household, we seek as informant whichever person is most able to answer the questions. You will be told whether it is the housewife or householder who has to be seen. In a sense your informant is chosen because of the role or position he holds in the family. You will always be told for such a survey which "role" member to seek out. You do not have to decide this for yourself.

The approach is not as easy as (a) since you have no name to lead you direct to the person you wish to interview.

Having established that whoever comes to the door is resident in that house, go on quickly to explain that you are uncertain who you wish to see, since you have not been given a name, but you have been asked to come to this address and see the "housewife/householder" (as applicable). Mostly this leads to the person saying either she is the one concerned or that it is her (– –). From that point on one pursues the chosen individual in the same way as for (a) type sample.

Note our use here of the words housewife and householder does no more than get you near enough to the right person. Informants will not know our precise definition of these terms and once you reach the chosen individual you need to check he is the housewife/householder in **our** terms. (See chapter 11 for definition.)

If the person is suspicious of your first question and asks why you want to know who is the housewife/householder there, it can help simply to say that you are from the Government Social Survey. Try to add no more until you have an answer which identifies the person you need to pursue.

37

(c) **Method of Identification of an Age or "Type" Person within a Population**

When we need to carry out studies on sections of the community such as the elderly or adolescents there are no registers available from which we can select these special sections of the population and so we mostly use the electoral register as a source of sample. Interviewers are asked to find out which of the addresses they have been given contain persons who are eligible by reason of being elderly or adolescent (according to our requirements).

At an address the way in which you find out if there are persons you wish to interview is by telling whoever comes to the door that you are uncertain who you wish to see, though you have been asked to come to this address, specifically. For the given survey you will then be told either to:-

i) Ask how many people there are living here above and below certain ages (you will be told to quote either the actual or a wider age band than that in which we are interested).

ii) Ask for a list of all persons living here, and in turn the ages of each of those persons.

Preface the above request by saying you are from the Government Social Survey. Do not explain the purpose of the survey until you have the answers to i) or ii). If people know the full reason for your visit before you have established eligibles anyone disinclined to be interviewed could easily say there are no people of the required ages, rather than admit that there are and then have to explain why they prefer not to participate. We cannot afford to 'lose' any eligibles as the sample becomes unrepresentative.

(Pursue anyone established as eligible on lines already discussed at (a) and (b).)

Ineligibles

Not all households (in c) will contain eligible persons. In cases where you establish that no-one in the household in to be interviewed, it is good public relations to thank the person who has given you the information and mention briefly that we are conducting surveys amongst people under or over a certain age. Calling on a cross-section of houses throughout all districts is the only way in which we can be sure of including all eligible people in an area. For the addresses at which no-one is eligible for the interview, a form noting that this is the case has to be sent by you to H.Q.

(d) Method of Approach when Identifying Whole Household

Some studies on patterns of expenditure necessitate participation of the group of people living at an address, since their expenditure may overlap. The group may be the natural unit for the study, e.g. a household for the study into expenditure on rent or other housing costs or expenditure on clothing.

So far we have said that one stands the best chance of gaining co-operation by seeking out the individual selected for the interview and making a personal plea for his co-operation.

When the whole household is meant to co-operate each member must be consulted, but your chances of success may depend on an observance of protocol.

Normally, the householder proves to be the father or husband at the address, and, in general, it is common throughout the country that the main male in the household likes to be consulted on matters affecting the family. It is wise on a first call at an address of this kind to say you have been asked to see all adults there, but in particular the householder. At which point one is usually told which member of the household that is. Having checked when he is likely to be in (although your informant will also be eligible for interview) try to leave over the explanation of survey purpose until the time you recall to see the group together. Often it will suffice at the first call to say you want the chance to explain fully to **all** the family the purpose of your visit without taking up one of the member's time now.

On any samples, if anyone tries to stop you from seeing eligible person(s) (excluding persons under 18 years) exercise polite persistence by saying you would nevertheless like to be given the opportunity of coming back to discuss the reason for your visit with the person concerned. You may feel it helps to add that you were asked by Headquarters specifically to meet the named person. But note that if, on any type of sample, a householder or family member gets to the point of actually refusing to let you enter the house now **or at any future date**, if he says this much, then you must not return.

Similarly, at a multi-household address (one containing different catering units) if the landlord meets you and says NO you cannot see his tenants, you cannot go against his wishes and re-enter the house.

Experience shows that some family members' fears as to the possible disinterest of their householder in surveys is usually illfounded. Often a wife is reluctant to make a definite appointment for you with her husband, but this is usually only a sign that, in general, a wife dislikes committing her husband to a definite appointment without his prior knowledge.

(e) Exceptional Approach to Specific "Special" Populations

Sometimes our surveys cover businesses, where we need to consult Managing Directors, or staff of some Public Service department, or inhabitants of an institution. Whereas the general population are given no prior notification of a study, on surveys where business and public bodies are concerned, permission from the appropriate authorities is first gained by Headquarters for entry to such premises. It is customary for introductory letters to be sent by us to the individuals concerned. The letters may quote that an interviewer will be telephoning to make an appointment to see the informant.

One should not expect to walk in on business people unannounced, hence the allowed use of the telephone on these special samples. It can be difficult putting over a survey purpose by this method and you should dissuade the informant from too much enquiry on the telephone. Try to make an appointment and explain that it will be easier to answer his questions in person.

Sample (a) to (e)

You will see from the above that a lot of care should go into establishing that you have the **right informant** and that you give yourself **the best chance of putting the survey purpose over to him in person.** The importance of this cannot be overestimated if you are to achieve a high response rate.

Once face to face with your informant, cover most of points (i) to (vii) (Page 33) briefly.

SPECIAL POINTS TO BEAR IN MIND WHEN CONTACTING INFORMANT

(i) Appointments

It is most important to keep any appointment that you make with the public. If you know you will be unable to keep an appointment either call earlier to cancel it, or else write to them if there is time. A semi-appointment should be binding and dealt with in this way on your part. On the other hand if the public break appointments you must accept it with good grace and try again on another day or evening.

(ii) Minors

Whatever the type of sample, if the person to be interviewed is a young person (under 18 years, living at home), permission of his parents or guardian must be gained before the interview takes place.

If on any such survey the parent or guardian wishes to be present at the interview the research officer concerned will tell you whether or not it is to be allowed or whether he prefers not to have an interview in such circumstances.

(iii) **Employees**

If your informant is an employee living in the employer's own home, e.g. a maid, gardener or housekeeper, then the employer's permission must be sought. In turn the employee must be told he is free to decide whether or not he wishes to participate. He does not have to do so simply because his employer has agreed to his being seen by you.

B *STAGE 2 OF CONTACT* (applicable to all types of samples (a) to (e))

After the "doorstep" contact, once inside the house you may well be asked by the informant to say what you have really come about. This does not mean, necessarily, that your doorstep explanation has been inadequate. It is probable that most people only half listen initially because they are preoccupied with thoughts of whatever was happening before the doorbell rang or they are making a judgment on whether or not to let you into the house.

Once inside the house repeat what you have said on the door-step, expanding on the topic of the survey and explaining more fully about sampling procedure or our organisation's bona fide nature, to an extent that will satisfy the informant. Say this much to him once inside the house, irrespective of whether or not you are asked to do so. Do not be lulled into foregoing explanations because a type of informant says *"come in"* straight-away and appears to trust you. You should cover yourself by making sure he knows where you are from.

Avoiding Misconceptions

All sorts of misconceptions may arise from an inadequate explanation. Sometimes the informant connects your visit with some circumstances in his private life of which you are totally unaware. For example, the informant may have been in hospital recently, or have applied for a pension or a house, and imme-diately assume that you have called because of this. Be on the alert for misunderstandings of this kind, as it is important to make the informant understand that there is no connection between any two events. Such an initial misconception might make the informant apparently more willing to give the interview, think-ing that it has some connection with his own affairs. But he is likely to be justifiably annoyed when he finds out during the course of the interview that it is not so. Also, the feeling that the interview is likely to have some bearing on a personal matter might direct him to answer the questions in a particular way which he feels would be to his advantage.

Authorisation Card

When in the house always show the informant the **authorisation card,** with which you are issued, and draw his attention to the

reverse side of it whereon is printed the statement about con-
fidentiality and the voluntary nature of the survey (points (v)
and (vi) page 33). It is a useful moment at which to say, for
example, *"As you will see from the back of the card, anything
said to us on any of our surveys is treated as confidential. It
also says that it is up to the public whether they wish to take
part"*, but having said this you must add at once *"The value of
our surveys lies in getting everybody's participation. And we
are grateful, as in your case, that you are helping us"*. Do
remember to take back the card once the informant has looked
at it since you need to show it in every house.

Though we advise showing the card in the house, exceptionally
it can be shown usefully on a doorstep if a timid person, perhaps
a woman living alone, is hesitant about letting you enter.

Putting Over the Purpose of a Survey

As a Government Department and a research unit concerned with
accurate data, we are most anxious that informants should be
clear on our objectives and under no misapprehension as to what
they are participating in.

You need to set the right tone for the interview by neither
blinding informants with science, talking down to them nor
making any unsubstantiated claims as to a study's purpose or
outcome.

Remember, no interviewer is expected, or should pretend
to be, an expert on the subject matter of the survey. If the
informant assumes you have specialist knowledge, point out that
this is not the case and that we are a research unit and deal with
many projects for different departments. You are basically a
reporter. In fact you will find that the wording of the questions
and instructions for the particular survey cover any technicalities
of the subject matter which you may need to know.

You are meant to study your instructions and take notes at
briefings when you are being told the background to the particular
survey. Then, in the interview, you will be able to give an
account of the purpose of the survey and the department commissioning it.

Survey Reports

One cannot guarantee survey findings will be made available to
the general public, since commissioning departments have the
right to decide this matter. Survey results are often published
as White Papers, and are available through public libraries.
Our findings are not used by the Government alone. Once published they may be used by anyone concerned with the field of
social research and the internal economy of Great Britain.

A General Explanation of the Purpose of Government Social Surveys

Irrespective of the subject matter of a survey one can introduce the study, in part, or answer questions about the value and use of such work, by explaining that surveys are valuable as a means of providing to Government Departments and public bodies information which they cannot get from other sources. A survey can provide an up-to-the-minute picture of some aspects of the way of life of members of the public. Or it can show their reactions to a government measure or any national issue.

The data thus collected is used to supplement other material already at the disposal of the Government Department commissioning the survey. Our findings can help decide some future policy matter, or help a department judge the effects of past policy. Similarly, in the case of a Royal Commission, data collected by the Government Social Survey would be incorporated in findings from other sources and go towards helping the commission make its recommendations.

Sometimes it is helpful to give the informants the above explanation in full, in other cases it will suffice to make the point that SURVEYS SERVE THE GOVERNMENT AS A WAY OF KEEPING DIRECTLY IN TOUCH WITH MEMBERS OF THE PUBLIC. That the public can voice their true feelings, or quote direct to the Government their own circumstances on the survey subject, is a point which appeals to many in the population.

Be ready to state that we have no link with political parties. We are within the Civil Service, and at a remove even from the commissioning department. We are a research unit and as such have no axe to grind. We cannot say what action may be taken by a Government Department as a result of any survey findings. We can guarantee to the informant, however, that our task is to present the truth of the matter and we will report the situation as it is expressed to us; there will be no distortion of facts or expressed opinions.

Interviewer Individuality in Survey Explanation

It may seem from the above that one is suggesting that you adopt a highly stereotyped approach to the public. This is so in respect of stating fully to an informant why he is being approached by us, but in order to get the understanding of all types of informants you will need to be extremely flexible in your choice of words and length of explanations.

For each survey, before working on it, you will need to think out several ways of introducing the survey to the public. You can emphasise a different facet of the survey purpose to suit different types of people. Adolescents, housewives, professional and retired persons would not all respond equally well to precisely the same introduction.

If people react rudely, which is rare, on no account react to the rudeness, but try to find out whether it hides fear or guilt; once you know to what a person objects or has concern about, you have a good chance of winning him over.

Overcoming Non-co-operation

For our surveys to be wholly representative of the population we need to achieve 100% response. In a sense your own part of the sample is deficit (that bit less representative) by each informant that you fail to interview.

Non-response can be due to:

(a) Death of your chosen informant, or demolition of the address at which we have asked you to call.

(b) Inability to find your informant at home because he is in hospital, goes out frequently, works long hours and in consequence has insufficient time to spare for an interview.

(c) Outright refusal to participate in surveys.

These categories form a minority of the sample set but are worth mentioning to show the problems of random sampling and to illustrate which non-contact you cannot avoid and which can be overcome to some extent with perseverance.

To (a) above, clearly, no blame is attached to the interviewer!

(b) the non-contact rate due to informants not being found at home can be reduced to hardly any, since a survey is usually in the field over three or four weeks. This means one has time to call back in different weeks to catch up with persons who were on holiday or in hospital on your first call. If you are prepared to put yourself out by calling many times on busy people and to fix appointments for a week or so ahead, in nearly all cases, ultimately, your informant will find time to give you an interview.

(c) Very few people are entirely unwilling to co-operate on surveys, **providing** they are offered a good explanation as to the purpose of the survey, re-assured on how they came to be chosen for interview and on the confidential nature of their participation.

However, you must appreciate the public's freedom to refuse us an interview, and not press anyone who states unequivocally that it is against his principles to take part in surveys: neither must you take advantage of a timid person's inability to put his fears and rejection of you into words, if you are aware that he cannot accept you.

It is important that you are convinced of the right of surveys before you ask for the public's co-operation, otherwise you might

44

imagine you see a refusal at a stage when an informant is showing only minor reluctance; perhaps not wishing to be bothered or by being diffident about his ability to help us.

Your tone with doubtful people needs to be matter of fact, pleasant, enthusiastic, reassuring and quietly persistent. It is only when you have said as much as you can to an informant on reasons for the study and reasons for bothering them, that you can be certain, if such is the case, that what we want is anathema to your informant. An unhappy *"not today thank you"* housewife, trying to shut the door, if left so remains unhappy and possibly more fearful of callers in future.

Tell her that you would like to explain the reason for your visit, and do so briefly but clearly. She may be relieved on realising there is nothing to fear about your call. Your effort at communicating with her may pay off in the sense that she confides her misconception, or fear of your call, and then gives you an interview.

Refusal Effect on the Interviewer

Real refusals are few, but the effect of a refusal on you, unless you take steps to avoid it, can be to debilitate. If it does lower your morale it can have the result that your dejection affects other people as you call on them and gets you more refusals, which are not genuine, but, which are caused by your own lack of confidence in what you are doing.

If ever you do have a refusal, afterwards think how you handled it.

(i)   How did you introduce yourself and the survey?

(ii)   Was your informant distraught at the time?

(iii)   Did you allow for his mood in what you said?

(iv)   Did you call at a socially unconventional time for the district in which you were working; either lunchtime or late in the evening?

(v)   Was there anything unconventional in the way in which you were dressed on that occasion?

If the answer is yes to any of these, then learn for the future what to avoid and so overcome the problem.

If you can see no reason for the failure, but neither can you accept it, write to the office or telephone your training officer to discuss the matter to see if we can offer a clue as to what went wrong. It could be that an adverse effect came from your choice of words; some emphasis given wrongly to one aspect of the study. Or it could be that the area in which you are working has suffered recently from burglars or door-to-door sales-men, which has left the public rife with suspicion, quick to pick out apparent oddities of callers. Remember you have said that you are working for a government research unit and the public may well have an image as to what any government representa-tive will be like. Whilst you cannot know and live up (or down) to their expectations you must take care to behave and look a responsible citizen, so they can accept you as a representative of the Government.

If you have spent considerable time talking to someone who decides not to participate after all, do assure them before leaving that we appreciate that we have no right to make people take part against their wishes, nor would we like them to do so. Indicate that we know the worth of our work is affected by "loss" of anyone from the sample, since it means we are not including in our research a complete cross-section if we are missing people such as themselves. This has been why you have been so anxious to see them.

In any case of a person saying he does not want to take part but giving no reason, end by telling him that you do have to account for all people you were asked to see. Ask him to say why it is that he prefers not to help, since we are interested in people's reasons.

This is the case, that we will want a full write up from you as to the approach you made and the actual reason for refusal.

Chapter 7

CONDUCTING THE INTERVIEW

The foregoing sets the tone of your contact with any informant.
However, your role in establishing a friendly atmosphere has
only just begun. Whilst your careful introduction of the survey
will mean your informant is prepared for some questioning,
if he is to be kept interested and his attention directed to the
subject of the survey for as long as is necessary, encourage-
ment and attention from you are called for as the questioning
proceeds.

Seating

Sit facing your informant whenever possible, so that he cannot
read the schedule or closely watch the answers being recorded.
If he becomes too aware of the form filling process the spontaneity
may go from his replies. Take care to sit facing the light for
deaf people so they may lip read if they want to. Get your
informant sitting comfortably; an elderly person should be
cajoled into sitting in his own chair rather than taking it yourself, if it is proffered. On the other hand if you have a busy
housewife in the midst of a chore such as ironing, she might be
happiest if encouraged to get on with her work, if she prefers,
whilst you talk to her.

Documents

In general it is best not to get schedules out until you have
entered the house, shown your card and had some sign that your
informant has accepted your presence.

Remember many people are unused to paper work and may
feel uneasy on sight of many papers. It is important to have
all papers to hand (but in your folder) when you enter the house
so that you can produce them in an unobtrusive way. Similarly,
have the necessary pencils and any prompt cards to hand to
avoid creating a hiatus on entry. If you had to search for
materials this would, wrongly, give a diffident informant time
to have qualms about his ability to help. People need leading
gently into the questioning and your efficiency in starting the
interview smoothly depends on your preparedness for it.

Interviewer Manner and Speech

Your interview does not begin with Q 1 on the schedule and end with the last question on it, rather it runs from the moment you enter the house until your departure from it.

If you are au fait with the subject matter of the survey, the order and the special instructions for each question, then during the interview you will have time, correctly, to concentrate on your informant's reaction to what you are saying. In any normal conversational situation, if one person never looked at the other the conversation would soon stop, and so it will in the interview situation if you fail to look expectantly at the informant for replies.

You need to deliver the questions distinctly, and additionally, if the person is at all deaf, loudly. Your tone of voice should be governed a little by your informant and the situation in which you are interviewing. If he has a soft voice, or if there are other people present, it helps to use a soft tone oneself to indicate you are talking confidentially to him, but remember to speak clearly throughout. Watch the informant and if he shows any sign of bewilderment or slight suspicion, give further explanation of the general object of the enquiry or, if the question is a factual one, give a reason for the particular question and its relevance to the subject matter of the survey.

Preambles

Several topics are covered in an interview and in order to help the flow of the questioning you can give a preamble when you are introducing a new topic. Without the use of linking phrases from you the informant may begin to feel the questions are never ending, yet with their use he can be kept interested and sense that you are moving toward the end of the interview.

If you mention to him that you are changing the subject a little (and why) it helps to avoid any upset in your relationship which could occur if the informant noticed himself that the nature of the questions was changing and he felt you had moved on to something unrelated to whatever you had said the survey was about.

A particular example of the type of topic it is necessary to introduce is one that occurs on all surveys under the heading of classification, where we are asking for background facts about the informant. You will have introduced your survey as being on behalf of a particular Ministry who is interested in either views or facts on a given topic. The informant has agreed to talk about this topic. However, unless he is familiar with survey techniques, he may not see the relevance of your asking him for details of who lives in his house, his occupation or his age last birthday, all of which you will need to ask at some stage in the interview. We need to have this data because in our surveys we aim to reproduce in miniature the characteristics of the whole population. We must relate our findings to many factors in the lives of our informants in order to discover which factors affect their opinions on the subject under enquiry: this much you must tell him.

Pace and Tone of Questioning

You need to keep an interview progressing at a pace to suit your informant. The speed at which you ask questions must be governed by the speed at which your informant talks and thinks out his answers, rather than by your own natural speed. Learn the schedule layout and partly memorise the actual wording of the questions before starting the interview. In this way you can faithfully ask the correct questions, but phrased conversationally. If questions are read in a natural tone, rather than read parrot-like, they will be better understood by your informant, and your task of creating a natural relationship will be easier.

Continue speaking clearly for the whole of the interview and take care not to speed up your questions when you are towards the end of your list of addresses. An informant is always hearing the questions for the first time so allow him plenty of time in which to answer, but do not allow the interview to drag. Remember not to talk too much yourself (other than in putting questions) and correctly avoid saying anything that could influence the informant's answers in any way. A few moments' silence whilst the informant thinks out an answer is often desirable. On the other hand, avoid long pauses which might irritate or embarrass him. A slight pause while you are writing down the answer will seem natural and must occur sometimes, since ALL THE ANSWERS MUST BE RECORDED AT THE TIME OF INTERVIEW.

Though the informant will see you are writing it is best not to draw his attention to the extent to which you are recording his responses. If, wrongly, you read out what he has said, he might start behaving differently by limiting replies because he is self-conscious or by reeling off soap-box statements because his ego prompts him to take the limelight.

Do not allow too much digression on the part of the informant between questions, but sense when it is very necessary to allow him to wax confiding and say something out of context of the interview. If all informants are kept too rigidly on the path of the interview, in some situations you will lose out on data because an informant may be bursting to describe some other experience to you. It may be only if he is allowed to tell you what he feels he must, that in turn your relationship will be deep enough to get the best from him for the rest of your questioning.

Role of the Interviewer

So far emphasis has been given throughout this chapter to the possible reaction of the informant to the interview. What of you in your role as interviewer?

Consider the situation. You are sent by us to meet people unknown to you. But when you meet them you are facing a situation common to you throughout your life. You have coped with endless encounters with strangers in trains, at work, at parties and you have entered into conversation with them.

Some conversations have no purpose other than to pass time pleasantly. Yet participants in many conversations aim to make them purposeful, they decide there are specific things they will find out of the other person. Other than when one is with friends the titles of the participants (e.g. doctor and patient) often indicate how purposeful the conversation is going to be and whether it is turning into an interview rather than an interchange of ideas.

When you meet your informant you make contact as one person to another. It is your subsequent words that begin to define the roles you wish to adopt with this stranger, so that he begins to see and accept his role as "informant".

You know that you are with the informant in a business situation to collect data and not to tell him much about yourself. Were you to talk about yourself it could have an effect on him; you might come to be seen as a special person and then his responses would differ, he might start giving special replies in order to please, gratify, or have some other effect on you. He might decide your roles were changing and you would find he had turned it into a discussion, or general conversation, so that you were led away from the specific line of questioning or, one could say, you would have lost "control" of the interview. The guide lines given earlier are meant to help you establish your role with the informant.

We want you to build up an informant's assurance during and as soon as possible in the interview. If he is at ease with you and satisfied as to the purpose of questions in should help his comprehension and result in greater accuracy of response.

We need you to show appreciation and interest in what your informant is saying in order to get his involvement at sufficient depth. Yet, you have the task of not getting personally involved with the informant because you must keep control of the line of questioning.

Chapter 8

SPECIAL CIRCUMSTANCES AFFECTING THE INTERVIEW

When to Interview the Informant Alone

Earlier, in discussing initial contact, we mentioned the
fact that you might meet other members of the family. It follows
that often they will be present in the house whilst you are interviewing an individual. There are some cases in which you should
try to arrange to conduct an interview alone with the informant.
You may be questioning him on matters that he does not discuss
with other members of the household, or you may be wanting
his opinion and his alone, uninfluenced by anyone else. However, since a considerable proportion of the population have
only one living room and many interviews occur in the evening,
it is difficult to arrange to see people alone. You can mention
to informants that it might be best if you could see them alone.
If you have explained that you want their views or to discuss
some subject which they know they do not normally discuss
with the family members, then they may go out of their way to
let you sit, perhaps in the kitchen, where you will be uninter-
rupted for the necessary hour or so.

When to Interview with Other People Present

If the information being collected is purely factual, such as
data on housing, ages of family members, or other classificatory
items there is no harm in a third person being present, so long
as he is in a close enough relationship to the informant for the
informant not to mind his hearing what you have to say. On
factual studies it may even be an advantage to have someone
else present, where the other person knows the facts rather
better than the informant, and can help provide data. Note you
can only enlist the help of someone sitting in if your informant
permits it. **In no case can you take factual information without
the informant's permission and/or when he is absent.**

There are certain cases in opinion surveys where an informant needs to have a family member present for reassurance
before he will have enough courage to say what he thinks. A
drawback of having anyone else present during an opinion interview is that it is so difficult for onlookers to keep from "helping"
your informant, by putting words into his mouth or bursting
out with some view of their own to which he voices agreement.
**Ideally, any question designed to find out the informant's opinion
must be answered by the informant only.**

If the informant is not alone when interviewed on an opinion
survey, you must try to ensure that the informant's answers
are influenced as little as possible by anyone else who may be

present. If a third party interrupts at all, you should explain as tactfully as possible, if it is the case, that at the moment you want only the views of the person being interviewed, but will be very interested to hear what the other person has to say afterwards. If this fails to prevent further interruptions, you must take care to record only those answers from the informant which were unprompted by a third party. It is fairly easy to exclude opinions expressed by the onlooker to which your informant does not react. But it is difficult in the case where the suggestion leads the informant to say *"I agree or think that too"*. If this happens you will have to record the intervention and your informant's subsequent response to it since it acted as a stimulus to him. In such cases you need to make a note beside the answer saying whether, in you judgment, the informant's response was a lip service one, or a genuine opinion awakened by the prompting.

It is always important to have good public relations established between the interviewer and people surrounding the informant. Members of the family who sit in on an interview cannot be wholly ignored by you and anyone coming in during the interview should get some explanation from you as to your presence, and why you are interviewing the informant rather than them. Unless you give people a role in this way they may adopt one which is not conducive to a good interview. If you appeal to them to let their relative answer alone (the appeal to be made very sweetly) it is often obeyed, especially if you explain the chance by which their relative came into the sample.

Odd Reactions to Overcome

Exaggeration

Occasionally an informant may want to present a false image to you. If it is natural for him to present a front in this way when he meets strangers then it will be natural for him to want to defend himself in the same way when you, as a stranger, approach him. For example, someone may hint at the wonderful job he has, and it can be cruel and hard for you to press for truth on the matter later in the interview without making him lose face.

Since you know the full range of your questioning when you meet, and he does not, you need to stem an informant's natural defence, before he goes far in fantasy. Get over to him, as opportunities occur from the doorstep onwards, that you want his help, but also that you are not **over** impressed by any of his words. Take his response in a matter of fact way and show that what will impress you is to know exactly what he thinks and precise facts about some aspects of his life. Indicate it does not matter what kind of view he holds, so long as it is truly his own. We are in no position to censure informants.

52

Untruth

If you are told something which you sense may be untrue, in that the tone or speed at which it is said conveys an informant's fear or guilt in some way, try asking the question again using a linking phrase *"Can I just check, I am uncertain whether I made clear what I meant to ask you"* (and then repeat the question carefully). Often this will give the informant the opportunity to overcome any doubt about stating the truth. Your tone will help show that you do not take it to be a question of any special significance, and the inference of your own mishandling of the question can be used by the informant to excuse himself from not having been clear on what you wanted. A question which pressurises an informant in some way should prompt you to reiterate, just as you would if asked if a given reply were acceptable, that if what he has said reflects truly what he thinks, or if it is a fact so far as he knows it, then it is the answer we want.

Facetiousness

Another tone which might be adopted by a minority of those you wish to interview is one where, whilst the informant nominally agrees to the interview, he is answering tongue in cheek. In fact your manner whilst explaining the survey purpose, and the way you probe for exact replies during the interview, will often serve to school an informant to the degree of responsiveness required, but if it fails and the informant continues in the same vein try one of two lines: to a facetious response adopt a facetious tone yourself to show you appreciate his sense of humour but probe to sort out whether his response is genuine in spite of the tone or not. If you have an extreme case where the facetiousness masks an unwillingness to participate, and you both know this, then you may find it necessary to tell the informant that if, really, he is not willing to take part, we would rather he said no than that both parties wasted time. Such cases are rare, but worth a mention here to illustrate to you that we are not interested in nominal, only meaningful, response. It is not necessary for your informants to respond in an utterly earnest fashion before one can say they are taking the matter seriously. Never expect informants to treat any subject matter in exactly the same degree of caution, frivolity or seriousness to match your own. On the other hand, do not let yourself be hoodwinked and left feeling you are wasting time on someone who just won't use the word no to you, though he had no intention of co-operating.

Ending the Interview

Always thank the informant at the end of an interview. The public do not have to take part in surveys. Our enquiries are on worthwhile matters but the public are still doing us a favour when they agree to give their time and express their views fully to us. Our aim is to leave them happy about the whole reason for the survey. Make sure everyone has the opportunity to ask further questions of you about the background to the survey, should they want to, before you leave the house. If they do not ask anything then you may find you can incorporate a little more about the value of the study and their participation as you give them your thanks.

If anyone asks if they will hear anything further about the interview or be called on again, you cannot give a categoric no, since we have known cases where, by chance, the same household has come up on another survey, and as a safeguard to the public, Government Social Survey staff do re-call on a percentage of the people interviewed in order to check that interviewers have dealt with them in a correct and polite way.

Always leave the informant with permission to return to check any item, in case you discover an omission once you have left the house. Your conduct throughout the interview should be aimed at making the interview as pleasant an experience as possible for your informant, so that he is left feeling willing to co-operate in the future on **any** other survey.

Leaflets

Often we produce leaflets which name our organisation, expressing briefly the objects of a survey and containing a few words of thanks to the public for their co-operation. Unless you are told to the contrary, these leaflets are not meant to be left with people when an appointment has been made. No leaflet can be designed to replace your verbal explanation of a survey's purpose which can be tailored by you to suit the individual.

Leaflets are to be handed out on completion of the interview. The leaflet is intended to stop people reconsidering and worrying over the purpose of your questions once you have gone. An exception to this rule on leaving leaflets when all contact with the household is at an end is on record keeping surveys. On any such survey, once the initial interview is completed, if you have persons or families keeping record books, which you must collect at a later date, leaflets are left along with the record books to act as reassurance as to the bona fide nature of your organisation.

Confidentiality of Schedules

If on any survey an informant asks to see the schedule, either to read it during, or it could be before, the interview, or if he asks you to leave it for him to fill in, explain you want an opportunity to talk with him and that you have notes for your own guidance but no forms as such for him to complete. DO NOT SHOW A SCHEDULE TO INFORMANTS AND **NEVER** LEAVE THEM IN A HOUSE AFTER AN INTERVIEW.

If you were to let the informants read schedules before answering the same it would make nonsense of some of our schemes of analyses; if the informant is unaware of the form the questioning will take it is unlikely he will consider his replies, other than in the terms of reference of each specific question and in the light of foregoing replies. He has no knowledge of what is yet to come and it is unlikely there can be any fabrication that would not reveal itself before the end of the interview. But were he to know the question sequence beforehand, it is possible that the knowledge of the questions would condition if not educate him to devise a set of answers that more readily hung together. We would be getting considered answers to sequences of questions as opposed to spontaneous replies to individual items. We want all informants alike to be conditioned, so far as is possible, by nothing more than the questions that have been asked to date.

For anyone who asks you to show him a blank schedule, spelling out to an informant the reason for not doing so in the way above is not recommended. Simply indicate you have a check list to remind you what to talk about, but it is not a form of questions in the sense in which he means and go on to say you want the chance to talk with him and get his spontaneous replies.

If any survey allows any exception to this rule, on not showing informants schedules, it would be made clear to you at a briefing for that particular survey.

Chapter 9

METHOD OF INTERVIEW

By structured or standarised interview we mean one in which
the questions are decided in advance and are framed with the
same words and put in the same sequence to all informants.
A structured interview is the type most commonly undertaken
by the Government Social Survey at the main stage of field work.
It is the type to which the instructions in the next three chapters
refer.

Basic Instructions

Apart from instructions specific to the subject matter of each
survey there are principles governing a structured interview.
Our aim is to teach you to identify main types of questions, to
become familiar with their format, knowledgeable in handling
the different types or sequences of questions and adept at
recording responses during the interview. When you are
familiar with all this you will thereby know when to stimulate
informants to give a full reply to any question and how to do
this in a way that will not over-influence them or alter the meaning of their response.

QUESTIONING

Asking the Questions

The research officer's instructions on how to deal with each
question must be carried out meticulously. Questions are tried
out by means of a pilot survey before the survey proper is
launched. **The wording and order of the questions are the
result of careful thought and experiment and, at the main stage
of a survey, in general neither the wording nor order of the
questions should be altered by the interviewer.** Were words
within questions changed it would mean in effect that the answers
to be analysed are answers to several different questions.

The importance attached to your understanding of the question
cannot be overemphasised. Frequently in these pages you will
be told to relate answers to the original question. This means
that you must know the scope of the question in order to decide
whether or not a given response fully answers it.

For example, if you had to pose the question:

.... Question – *"Do you like eggs?"*

and you received the following answer – *"I do not like boiled
eggs"*,

your question may or may not have been answered. The informant may not like eggs at all, or he may have lost sight of the question and have thought, and told you, of a method of cooking eggs which produced a flavour he disliked. Since his answer could be taken in one of two ways you would have to repeat the question stressing *"eggs"*.

Whereupon the answer may be

...... *"Yes I like them cooked certain ways"* or

...... *"No, I hate them whichever way they are cooked, but especially when they are boiled."*

This is not to say the interviewer must exercise her own prejudices and decide an answer is not acceptable because she disagrees with it personally. However, you are in the best position to decide the category of response, providing you remain unbiased, because you can take up a response and ask for further explanation (as in the above example) in order to clarify it and categorise it correctly. It follows that you have to take the responsibility of noting failure of any question; of seeing when an informant truly has no response.

A correct judgment of response will only come if you know the aims and type of question being used. Some questions seek a reply in exact terms; a complete reflection of the informants views or a full statement of the facts. Other questions are aimed at producing an answer in more general terms, so that we get an overall assessment of opinion or the facts within a given range. An explanation of the types and functions of questions you will use for the Government Social Survey follows.

The Function of Questions

Irrespective of the type of data sought, a question, if it is a good one, should be as simple and universally comprehensible as is consonant with conveying the required meaning. The meaning we wish to convey can be fairly complex.

From reading (or hearing) a question it is not always easy to decide whether a factual answer or an opinion is being sought. **The purpose for which the question is put determines whether it is to be handled as fact or as a matter of opinion (or attitude).** It is necessary for the research officer to clarify for you the purpose of each question, because the way you handle the question will depend on whether one seeks a factual reply or an expression of opinion or knowledge.

PURPOSE OF QUESTIONS

(a) **To ascertain FACTS**

Basically there are two kinds of Factual questions:

1 Those about a situation as it exists at the time of interview (observational and classificatory data).

2 Those about past events; namely memory data.

EXAMPLE 1 OF A FACTUAL QUESTION
(From SS. 815A Family Expenditure Survey)

Q. Does any member of your household get
free or concessionary coal or coke?   No 2
Yes 3

The question should be asked of the informant as it is written on the schedule. This is the form in which it has been tried out on the pilot and adopted for the main survey because it contains the most meaningful and universally understood words. After using the original question you must judge whether or not the answer, as given, is an answer within the original terms of reference of the question. If it is not, and your informant has clearly misunderstood what was required of him, use the definition of the question (which you are given in the instructions for that survey) to add to the question wording to make the point of it clear to your informant.

Occasionally, as in the classification section, factual questions will not be written out in full on the schedule. This is the case in example 2 (given opposite). Note the precision of items (a) to (e), all are included so we shall get exact data on the cost of gas and electricity. But note, before asking (a) you would need to use your own question *"Do you have mains gas and/or electricity"* before you could code 1, 2, 3, or 4 and before you would know whether you needed to go on to the supplementary questions (a) to (e).

EXAMPLE 2 OF SEQUENCE OF FACTUAL QUESTIONING
(From SS.815A Family Expenditure Survey)

GAS AND ELECTRICITY

	Gas	Electricity	Period	Office Use	Amount £	s	d
THESE CODES APPLY TO GAS OR ELECTRICITY BOARD SUPPLIES							
None	1	5					
Slot meter	2	6					
Account meter	3	7					
.... Other, specify	4	8					

IF CODES 2 OR 6 APPLY (SLOT METER)

	Amount of rebate	D.K.					
(a) If you get a rebate when the meter is cleared, how much was it last time?	Gas.	1	......		....	....	
	Electricity.	2	......		....	....	

IF CODES 3 OR 7 APPLY (ACCOUNT METER)

	Quantity	D.K.					
(b) Can you tell me what quantity of gas or electricity your last account covered?	Gas (therms)........1		......		....	....	
....	Electricity (units)....2		......		....	....	

	Payments for						
(c) How much did you pay for gas or electricity in that account including standing charge and meter rent but excluding hire, hire purchase and maintenance?.........	Gas		....		....	....	
	Electricity		......		....	....	

	Hire of appliances						
(d) How much did you pay for the hire of gas or electric appliances in the last account, excluding any hire purchase?	Gas		......		....	....	
	Electric		......		....	....	

HIRE PURCHASE PAYMENTS SHOULD BE ENTERED IN SCHEDULE C.

	Maintenance of appliances						
(e) How much did you pay for maintenance in the last account?	Gas		......		....	....	
	Electric		......		....	....	

(b) To ascertain opinion (attitude) or knowledge

An opinion question is designed to discover the **informants'** views on or evaluation of the subject matter of the question.

A knowledge question assesses the extent of the informants' knowledge of or information about a given topic.

On Opinion and Knowledge questions it is essential that you use the actual form of words given on the schedule, in their entirety, and that you do not attempt to interpret them. This is because the difference between opinion (including knowledge) questions and those to be handled as factual is that the former are quoted in reports as the informant's own response and thereby his interpretation of a given form of words (namely the question). It is necessary to present the results in this way because it is known that even slight alterations in the wording of opinion questions, which may make no apparent difference to the sense, can have an effect on the replies given to them.

The results of factual questions are not usually presented as responses given to certain stimuli, as in the case of opinion questions, but as facts about the number of people spending given sums of money, taking different kinds of education or living in types of dwellings.

It has been said above that you must use a given opinion question in its entirety. It follows that as you are not allowed to explain the question you must put it with care to the informant. If it is a question that sounds like one used before but it is one in which the concept is different, pause before delivering it, and make sure you give the right emphasis to it (as instructed at the survey briefing).

If the informant mishears or misunderstands the question, in the sense that he answers entirely off point, you should repeat the question again in its entirety. If he does not answer when the question has been repeated, or if he makes a comment to the effect that he does not understand, or considers it a silly question, record this on the schedule and proceed to the next question.

EXAMPLE 3 OF OPINION OR ATTITUDE QUESTION
(From SS 379 Women's Employment)

Q. *"What do you think are the attractions for married women in going out to work?"*

o

EXAMPLE 4 OF KNOWLEDGE QUESTION
(From SS 353B Smoking and Health)

Q. *"Do you think that during a year more people die in road accidents or from lung cancer?"*

o   Road accidents 1
                                      Lung cancer 2

Having asked an opinion question you may be asked by an informant for your views on the subject or for an explanation of what you meant by it. If asked what you think about it yourself say that you have not thought much about it, or reiterate that you are interested to hear his view. If asked what an opinion questions means, practise the art of turning back a question to the informant and say it means whatever he takes it to mean (but write his query as well as the subsequent answer on the schedule).

If, wrongly, you attempted to interpret an opinion question, you would be educating people in some way on that question and influencing the direction of their reply. Look back to example 3 (page 61). If the informant asked you *"what do you mean by attractions?"* If you tried to explain by using a synonym, perhaps saying "what do you think they 'like' about going out to work" you would be altering the concept of the question. We would neither know what the original question meant to your informant nor, since we would not know your question, would we know how your interpretation differed from what the question was meant to convey.

Sometimes an informant asks you for facts about yourself; from which district you come, whether you have children, which school they go to and whether you work as an interviewer every day. If you are on an opinion enquiry it may affect the informant's subsequent responses if you give him facts about yourself. Consider example 3 again; you might ask this question of someone who disapproved of women who had children of primary school age going out to work. If this was a question he had asked of you and it happened that you had children of this age then when you came to ask this question the informant might not spell out his disapproval because he did not wish to offend you personally.

Methods used in collecting data of factual and attitudinal nature

Types of question

1 OPEN Questions

An open question is one which, from the form of the question, gives the informant no notion of the way you want or expect him to reply, except within the terms of reference of the original question.

EXAMPLE 5 OF OPEN QUESTION
(From SS 369A Local Government Councillors)

Q. *"Looking back on the time you have spent so far as a councillor, what are the things which have given you most satisfaction?"*

O

Open questions, such as the example given above, are used when a full investigation of various aspects of the informant's thinking is required.

In example 5 you would accept as the answer anything which the informant mentioned, which could be considered within the terms of reference of the original question, i. e. whatever he mentions as having given him most satisfaction whilst he has been a councillor. The form of the question gives no clue as to what sort of things we would expect would give him satisfaction. Therefore the question is said to be "open" for him to answer according to his own interpretation of the words.

CLOSED (forced choice) Questions

Contrarily in a "closed" or "forced choice" question one is directing the informant's attention to a specific area and laying down the terms in which you want him to reply.

EXAMPLE 6 OF CLOSED OR FORCED CHOICE QUESTION
(From SS 343A.   Cross National Survey – Older People in
Q.   Great Britain)
Does a doctor visit you regularly
or occasionally, or only when
he is sent for?

Regularly 1
Occasionally 2
Only when sent for 3

Had we chose to ask example 6 as an open question it would have read *"How often does the doctor visit you?"* and we would have had disparity of reply, in that some people would have given number of visits per month, and others would have used phrases which were uncomparable, e.g. "sometimes", "often", "once in a while". We know the kind of frequency and distinctions in which we are interested therefore they are suggested to the informant.   He has to choose one of the three categories.

There are several reasons for using forced choice questions.

(i)   They may be used to lead in to a topic, to mention it in terms that are both general and familiar to everyone. In this way diffident informants who might feel that they had nothing to say if they were asked only open questions gain confidence. They do not have to find their own words, but only quote back some of those that you have used in the question. Once they have participated by giving an answer it encourages them to continue and respond freely on later open questions.

(ii)   Often a forced choice question would be used to demonstrate our impartiality on a topic. The inclusion of clear opposites in the choice of replies would demonstrate our willingness to accept any viewpoint. If informants can see you show no censure then they are more likely to choose the reply that most closely represents their true feelings.

(iii)   Within the body of the interview it is necessary to direct all informants to answer in the same terms on some specific aspects of the area under discussion for purposes of comparison. Since open questions are designed to give the informant freedom to answer in a variety of ways, the answers obtained from them may not be wholly comparable unless taken in conjunction with some forced choice questions.

Forced choice, SCALING QUESTIONS

In exploring opinions it is necessary to use more than one question because we may want to explore many facets of our informant's attitude and also because it may be difficult to place reliance on the replies to any one question. When a question is tried out on many people there will be some who simply do not see the implication of the question or who put a wrong interpretation on it, in other words the dimension that the informant gives to the question is not always clear from the reply. One technique for overcoming this difficulty is to use forced choice alternatives on a grand scale, i.e. to employ a whole battery of such questions, which are then analysed as a group.

When using such questions their reliability in the face-to-face situation may not necessarily be apparent to you. For they do not appear to reflect absolutely the informant's feelings on the matter. The point is that the replies to such questions are to be analysed in a battery. We can ask lots of questions of lots of people to counterbalance the degree of unreliability of interpretation of these questions by some people.

By considering the replies together in this way we can see how people did interpret each question by seeing the thread that runs through several of the questions. By this method we can separate out different dimensions of reply, and the unreliability of response can be cut by not relying on one or two questions only. In other words, it can be argued that by scales we do justice to the complexity of attitudes on a topic, and in turn compensate for the inevitable unreliability which attaches to some kinds of questions.

EXAMPLE 7 OF SCALING QUESTIONS
(From SS 353B Smoking and Health)

Q. *"I would like to tell you just a few things people are saying about lung cancer and smoking, and see how far you agree or disagree with them."*

(a) "There are other causes of lung cancer – such as fog and fumes – which are more important than smoking

..... (Do you) Agree Strongly......... 1
Agree Mildly 2
Neither Agree nor Disagree 3
Disagree Mildly 4
(or) Disagree Strongly?"........ 5

(b) 'It has been proved that smoking causes lung cancer....... (Do you) Agree Strongly......... 1
Agree Mildly 2
Neither Agree nor Disagree 3
Disagree Mildly 4
(or) Disagree Strongly?" 5

(c) "The experts differ among themselves about lung cancer and smoking
..... (Do you) Agree Strongly 1
Agree Mildly 2
Neither Agree nor Disagree 3
Disagree Mildly 4
(or) Disagree Strongly?" 5

Handling Scaling Questions

If part of an interview has been conducted by the use of open questions (page 63) where the informant has been encouraged to respond fully and at length, when you move on to forced choice questioning your informant's pattern of response has to be changed.

Unless you explain to the informant a little of the way in which these questions are to be treated he may feel frustrated by questions that do not allow him to reply freely. Explain that in asking him to say whether he agrees or disagrees on the whole with the following statements, you realise that you are not allowing him to explain in detail his true feeling on this particular aspect of the subject. We are interviewing thousands of people, and we want to ask for their agreement or disagreement **on the whole** on this aspect of the survey. In aggregate, these approximations will express shades of feeling on a topic.

With some informants it is not necessary to give this reasoning. But it is still necessary to indicate that you want them to respond in a different fashion from previously. If there is a whole group of forced choice questions and the response we require is on a 5-point scale, running from a statement of complete agreement to utter disagreement (see example 7 opposite), which in the original schedule covered a further five statements then it is usual for us to provide a prompt card, (see page 70) listing the categories of response re degree of agreement or disagreement. You hand the card to the informant at the beginning of the section and tell him that you want him to reply in one of the given ways to each of the statements that you are about to make.

In order to get through these questions at a reasonable speed and not to overtax the informant or yourself, it may be helpful if you frequently explain that you would like him to give his opinion **on the whole.**

When you are asking *"Which of these opinions comes nearest to your own. . . ? "* If the informant declines to choose any of the opinions as *"nearest to his own"* the **first** time the question is put, or if in response he starts to give a long qualified statement which does not fit exactly within the terms of any one precode, you should follow up with an *". . (and) (so) which of these opinions would you say comes* **nearest** *to your own?"* If the informant finds it impossible to generalise you will have to code the appropriate *"Don't know/No opinion"* category (code 3 in example 7) and write in his qualified statement by way of explanation, whenever the research officer has indicated that this is required.

In example 8, agreement or disagreement with five statements is sought. The technique explained above is to be used. You ask the informant to say *"on the whole"* whether he agrees or disagrees with each statement in turn. It is important to give equal emphasis to each item as you read it out, and to all parts of each question, so that there is no confusion about which statement the informant agrees on. Having read out the preamble *("I am going to read etc.")* and item 1, you would then say *"I would like you to tell me whether or not you feel the same way about (item) or not"*. Then read out and ask of item 2 in the same way. Before putting item 3 you would need to go back to the preamble and say *"another thing that parents have said about their children's school is (item 3)"*. Unless you refer back to the preamble in this way from time to time you will find the informant finds it difficult to give his agreement or disagreement because he no longer sees the statement in perspective.

Remember to introduce the remaining questions as being of a rather different nature once you reach the end of a scaling section. Otherwise, if open questions follow, you may not get open responses when you want them.

3 PROMPTING A prompt is any implicit or explicit suggestion of a possible answer or answers to a question.

The term prompting means suggesting an answer in some way. We may want to draw the informant's attention to the various possible answers, in order to define the meaning of the question more precisely, and make it easier for him to answer at the start of an interview.

Prompting may be necessary when questions involve a considerable feat of memory. On some expenditure types of survey the research officer may know that he risks loss of data from memory faults. He may circumvent this by instructing you to prompt at some point in the interview.

Putting words into people's mouths as you do when you suggest items to them is a dangerous practice. **PROMPTING, therefore, should only be done at the research officer's request.** He will know at which point he may have started to influence people's answers and take account of this in his analyses. Whereas, he will not know, or be able to make allowance for, an interviewer's own personal decision to prompt.

On "structured" interviews, where given responses are going to be subjected to statistical analysis, it is important that there should be as little variation as possible between one interviewer and another as far as method of interviewing is concerned. We use the same schedule of questions in each interview on a particular survey, and take steps to ensure that the schedule is handled in the same way in every interview by all interviewers. If you do not follow the correct instructions on when and when not to prompt, the data you collect will not be comparable with that of other interviewers.

Types of Prompt

There are two ways of handling a prompt:

(i)   In each case a list of prompts, i.e. precoded items,
       will have been provided on the schedule, possibly as
       part of the question. One way of handling this list is
       to go straight through it and treat it as a RUNNING
       prompt (example 9 opposite). The list should be read
       out clearly, taking care not to go too fast for the infor-
       mant, yet not pausing between items. An informant
       then has to choose one item out of many to which you
       have given equal emphasis. If you wrongly pause after
       one or two of the items you will get a different distribu-
       tion of replies from other interviewers, since your
       informants will have had a narrower range of possible
       answers suggested to them than the range which the
       research officer supplied.

(ii)   The other method is to treat the list as an INDIVIDUAL
       prompt (example 10) because a reply is needed to each
       item. The latter form of suggestion really amounts
       to a whole set of questions; you put item (i) to the
       informant, get an answer, then read out the preamble
       plus item (ii) get an answer, and so on to item (vi).

Prompt cards

In some cases the form of words in which we want the informant
to reply is printed on a card which can be handed to him. In all
cases where such a prompt is printed for the informant to read
you must explain the use of the card when you hand it to him.

Have these cards ready to hand so the questioning is not inter-
rupted. Explain that here is a list of items we would like him
to consider in turn, from which he is to choose one (depending
on purpose of prompt, see earlier examples). Tell him that
we want his reply expressed in one of the ways printed on the
form. Watch out for poor sight or lack of reading ability,
neither may be mentioned readily by the informant, but if you
see the card is not understood re-explain its purpose and read
out the items.

Identifying 'Prompted' questions

In identifying questions to be prompted on a schedule usually you will see the term "prompt" printed beside any responses that we want read out. Unless you see the word "prompt" the items are only meant to be read out if they are clearly part of the question, as in the following example.

EXAMPLE 9 OF A (RUNNING) PROMPTED QUESTION
(From SS 353 Smoking and Health)

Q. *"Could you say whether you think smoking is* ....

	Definitely a cause of lung cancer 1
(RUNNING)	may be a cause but it hasn't been proved... 2
(PROMPT)	is probably not a cause 3
	or is definitely not a cause of lung cancer?" 4

(Do not Prompt)   No opinion either way 5

EXAMPLE 10 OF (AN INDIVIDUAL) PROMPTED QUESTION
(From SS 366 Social Welfare for the Elderly)

Q. *"Do you usually have any difficulty"*   Yes   No

I N		(i) Going out of doors on your own? ......Y ... X
D	P	(ii) Going up and down stairs on your own? 0 ... 1
I V	R O	(iii) Getting about the house on your own? .. 2 ... 3
I	M	(iv) Getting in and out bed on your own? ... 4 ... 5
D U	P T	(v) Washing yourself? .... 6 ... 7
A L		(vi) Bathing? .... 8 ... 9

4 PROBING A probe is any stimulus which is not a prompt, applied in order to obtain a response from an informant, or a more extensive or explicit expression of it.

We want to give the informant every opportunity of saying all he wishes to say whenever a question is intended to allow him this opportunity. Often we want his spontaneous response and for you not to suggest possible answers to him.

When a research officer asks an opinion question he wants to be absolutely certain that exactly the same question was asked of all informants and that no new question was introduced by you of which he is unaware. It may be important to him to know how many people were unable to express an opinion at all in response to a given form of question. Obviously he will not know the question does not work if you explain it or change it without his knowledge.

The research officer will decide which questions on the schedule are to be handled as opinion questions and will make clear to you which these are before you work on the survey. In general he will mark these questions with an "O". (See foregoing examples 3 and 5.)

Once an opinion question has been asked you may be faced with an answer which needs clarifying before it is wholly under-standable, or it may be clear from what is said that the informant has misheard or misinterpreted the question. Any steps you take to clarify an answer, or to elicit further information, without suggesting an answer, are known as "probing". It is in the process of probing that the interviewer is most likely to introduce some form of bias unless care is taken.

An expectant glance or encouraging grunt from you after an informant ceases to reply can be as effective as words in letting an informant know that you want him to go on expressing his views or clarifying a factual response. Interested and quizzical looks must not be overdone, as this might make the informant simulate more interest in the subject than he has in order to gratify you.

There are some occasions when the informant takes no notice of such a form of probing and words are necessary. In order to avoid bias when there is need to resort to word-probes **you must take care to convey neither positive nor negative opinions on the subject under discussion**. It is possible to create or change opinion in the process of gauging it, and similarly there is the risk of educating the informant whilst trying to measure knowledge. The procedure for probing for opinion differs there-fore from that for factual questions.

72

PROBING OPINION QUESTIONS

Having put the question it is to be expected that it will be
sufficient stimulus to some people to elicit a full response;
an outpouring of their attitude toward the given topic. However,
they may,

    (a) use words that have one of two meanings

    (b) use phrases that are meaningless

    (c) be reticent on the subject.

To enable us to analyse answers, the given answers need
to be self-explanatory. At the time of interview you will have
to query any ambiguous statement from the informant and find
out exactly what he means. In turn it is necessary to encourage
him to answer as fully as he feels able to do.

It is difficult for you to think of unbiased phrases to use as
probes in the interview situation, therefore we have certain
**stock phrases to be used on all opinion questions that need
probing.** You must not invent your own phrases.

The phrases and the situations in which you are to use them
on opinion probing follow.

There are two kinds of probe:

    (a) **Clarifying,**   when it is necessary to find out what an
                     informant means by an ambiguous statement
                     that he has made, or when he has spoken
                     implicitly rather than explicitly (covered
                     by items (a) and (b) above).

    (b) **Exploratory,** when determining the extent or number of
                     opinions an informant can express on the
                     question topic (see (c) above).

PROBING KNOWLEDGE QUESTIONS

Knowledge probing is handled as above. When you are asking
for an explanation of an ambiguous answer, if it becomes clear
on a knowledge question that the informant is becoming vague
or incoherent because he really does not know the answer,
stop probing.

(a) **The phrases to be used as clarifying probes are:**

(i) *"Can you explain a little more fully what you mean by that?" or "Can you explain a little more?"*

(ii) *"In what way?"*

(iii) *"How do you mean (then quote word/phrase they have used which needs clarification)?"*

EXAMPLE OF CLARIFYING PROBE USAGE

If we consider the question used as example 3 on page 61.

Q. *"What do you think are the attractions for married women in going out to work?"*

A typical answer sequence might go as follows:

A. *"Oh they enjoy it".*

Q. *"Can you explain a little more fully what you mean*
(probe) *(by enjoy it)?"*

A. *"Well they enjoy the company, working with other adults instead of being alone in their home all day and it's a help."*

Q. *"In what way (is it a help)?"*
(probe)

A. *"The money is very useful, the cost of living being as it is most men's wages need supplementing by the wife's earnings. Really I think it's good for you."*

Q. *"How do you mean ('good for you')?"*
(probe)

A. *"As I've said, you get out and meet other people — it's better than being alone all day. It gives you a new interest and stops you being bored and it makes you feel independent of your husband, you don't have to ask him for every pound you want to spend."*

In the above sequence each of the variations of the explain probe has been used, but one could have used the "explain" phrase on at least two if not three of these items. The "explain" phraseology (i) is the one to use **most often** because it is the widest probe and, as you will see, sometimes it results in more than one item being given. You will see that without use of these clarifying probes the informant would have stopped talking much sooner and we would have lost ideas that she had on the subject. The precise meaning of the items she did volunteer initially was not apparent until probed. We could not have interpreted her statements to the effect that *"they enjoyed it"*, *"It's a help"* or *"It's good for them"*.

74

(b)   **The phrases to be used as exploratory probes are:**

(iv)   *"Is there anything else?"*

(v)   or *"Are there any other (reasons) (items)?"*

The "anything else" (iv) probe has to be used in conjunction with reference back to the question if the informant has been talking at length on a specific point of interest to himself. To say simply "anything else" may prompt him to think about something further to do with his last point and so get him talking at a tangent. If you need to refer back to the question then repeat the question in full.

The form *"Are there any other (reasons) (items)?"* (v) is used only where the original question incorporated the words reasons or items.

EXAMPLE OF EXPLORATORY PROBE USAGE

To take again our example question 3 (page 61), about the attractions for married women of going out to work. As you will see on page 74 the use of the clarifying probe has served a two-fold purpose. It has resulted in clarification of items already mentioned and it has served to encourage the person to go on to mention another item in each case. But after the final *"How do you mean?"* probe, you must ensure that the informant has had time to express **all** her ideas on the subject now that she has begun to think about it. You need to follow with the exploratory probe (i.e. either (iv) or (v)).

Several clarifying probes have been used in our example. Were you then to ask blandly *"is there anything else?"* probably the informant would say NO because the original question has been forgotten. Since you want to use the exploratory probe you must relate it to the original question as follows:

Q.   *"Are there any other (attractions for married women in going out to work)?"*

If the informant had answered unambiguously when the original question was put to her and had said in answer to your original question

A.   *"Oh they enjoy being at work because they are working with other adults instead of being alone in their home all day"*

one would have gone on to ask a straight *"Is there anything else?"* without bothering to repeat the question, since the question would have been fresh in her mind at that point.

Note the exploratory probe only relates to a question which asks for all ideas or reasons on a subject. If this question had been *"What is the main attraction for married women in going out to work?"* one would not probe for *"anything else"* because anything else would be superfluous in the terms of reference of the question.

You must keep the original question firmly in mind whilst you are probing.

It is only relevant to probe if, by so doing, you stand a chance of getting a fuller, clearer or more detailed response to the original question.

EXAMPLE OF (RELEVANT) PROBING

Consider the question given, example 5 (an open question) on page 63.

Q.   *"Looking back on the time you have spent so far as a councillor, what are the things which have given you most satisfaction?"*

to this question might come the answer

A.   *"My committee work I suppose."*

Q.   *"Can you explain a little more fully what you mean by*
(probe) *that?"*

A.   *"Well, I've been on the Housing Committee 5 years now and on the Welfare Committee nearly as long."*

This is a point at which you need to think of the aims of the question before you can decide how to probe further.

If you remember the question accurately you will take line (a) (below), if you think only of the given answer, and forget that you want to know what this means in relation to the question, wrongly you would go on to line (b).

proceed: correctly (a)	wrongly (b)
Q. (probe) *"In what way(s) have these things given you most satisfaction?"*	**Q.** (probe) *"Can you explain that a little more fully?"*
A. *"Well we've not done so badly. I'm interested in both these fields and by being on the committees I've managed to push through a lot of improvements in local services to the public."*	**A.** *"I got elected on to the committee when I'd only been a councillor a year or so and that makes it nearly five years."*
Q. probe) *"Are there any other things which have given you most satisfaction looking back on the time you have spent so far as a councillor?"*	**Q.** (probe) *"Anything else?"*
	A. *"No, I'm not on any more committees."*
A. *"Well I was made the mayor that's an honour really."*	
Q. probe) *"Anything else?"*	
A. *"No."*	

By which stage on the above example, procedure on (a) has produced a number of relevant points, which can be taken as answers to the original question. The procedure on line (b) has taken you away from the point of the question.

Once sight of the question is lost probing is irrelevant.

THE IMPORTANCE OF USING STANDARD OPINION PROBES FULLY CANNOT BE OVER-EMPHASISED. Analysis of interviewers' trial work shows a distinct difference in the quality and quantity of data collected by interviewers who probed fully and those who did not. Perfunctory use of standard opinion probes is not intended; you should continue using them up to a point at which your informant, by word or expression, clearly shows he has nothing more to say on the subject. Only **you** will be able to judge when this point has been reached in the individual interview.

Guard against over probing; if it is clear from the tone of the informant's last remark that he has now turned his thoughts right away from the question, then to ask him to tell you *"anything else"* may make him feel you do not understand that he has said all he has to say on the matter. To be over forceful is to make informants feel you want an answer at any price, and they will usually oblige in the end, but it is doubtful whether replies forced from people are reflections of true opinions.

No set rules can be given on when you have probed enough. It will depend on the individual and his responses, and you must accept that some informants will say they have no opinion and mean it, whilst others will start off saying they do not really know anything about the subject, as an opening gambit, whilst they think of a way of expressing what is in their mind.

Informant's Reaction to Probing

The informant may be embarrassed or depressed because he does not know very much, and you should make it clear that your concern is to have him say only what he does know or think. Get over to him that you are in no position to censure him and if need be mention that many people find it difficult to put their feelings into words. It may help to say that you are certain you would find it hard to answer questions on the spur of the moment if asked them. Having acknowledged his predicament in this way you must give him time to answer.

Probing on a knowledge question may lead to an informant asking you to tell him what the right answer is in order that he may know whether he is right or wrong. This situation must be handled with tact. Giving the informant information may bias the answer to a later question or alter his reaction to all further questions. If you supply answers he may take you to be an authority on the survey topic, and in consequence be loth to hazard answers that he thinks you may regard as uninformed. If you are asked if an answer is the right one, it is best to say either that you are not really sure yourself (which may be the case), or that probably you have been given a note about it, and if he so wishes you can look it up when you have finished discussing the other points you have in mind. This way you run no risk of making the informant feel inferior.

PROBING FACTUAL QUESTIONS

If there is an answer to a question that exists as an external truth then you are aiming to record that actual answer. This is what we mean by a fact. If your informant cannot provide the answer because he does not know it, it may be that some other member of his household does and your informant can get the fact from the other person whilst you are there. Sometimes people do not give you the actual answer immediately because they are unaware that you want a precise reply, in which case you will need to probe for it.

Proceed as follows on factual questions:

(i)   Always aim for the actual sum or figure.

(ii)   If it is not given immediately probe for it, and if that fails

(iii)   probe for an estimate or approximation. If this is the best that you can get enter the figure with an "e" (to the left of it) to show that it is not an actual figure.

(iv)   Only settle for a "don't know" (D. K.) if your informant, after careful probing on the matter by you, is unable to give an estimate.

The right kind of probe to use on factual questions may depend on the specific question and the research officer's instructions on the amount of detail he requires in answer to that particular question.

Probing on factual questions is left mainly to your discretion but remember:

(a)   to use "open" type questions, i.e. those that do not suggest an answer to the informant but ask him to think of the actual figure, if he can.

(b)   Avoid assuming you know the exact answer from any semi-statement by the informant. If you are probing for the total cost of a purchase, or querying how many people are in the house, or the number of children there, it may quicken the process if you help to sort out his replies, by jotting down items as he mentions them. You can then say *"I make the total so and so, does that sound right to you or not?"* This is an open enough form of check question to serve as a probe if necessary. It gives the informant the chance to refute the total and work out a more accurate one if he so wishes.

Memory Questions

Informants may have special difficulty in remembering required facts. For example on an expenditure type survey we may want to find out what purchases have been made over a period of time. Or on an employment survey we may want to know a date on which an informant left a former employer. You would be left recording on the schedule a DK (meaning "don't know") if you took some informants' original replies at face value, but you should go on to try to elicit accurate responses by careful probing.

People are not out to falsify data, but they do have their own biases in the recollection of events, tending to remember only things they want to remember or deem it important to remember. Unless we adopt a specific procedure when there are memory difficulties probing could so easily become prompting, i.e. suggesting. If you suggest to the informant a probable date of purchase or job-change, in what is to him a stress situation, (i.e. if he is trying to remember but cannot) he may grasp at your suggestion and accept it, because trying to remember has become a strain and he wants to stop thinking about it.

On memory questions you need to have a calendar to hand from which you can pick out the dates covering the period over which you want the informant to think back.

If we are concerned with a period of one month it would be of little use to say to the informant that you want him to think back over one month without specifying whether you meant 28 days or a calendar month. A "month" may mean more or less time to him.

Start by asking him to think back over the period, to whichever date you have as the starting point. Help him by advising him to consider, perhaps, each week in turn. Generally go back in time, i.e. from here and now back through last week then a fortnight ago, three weeks ago and so to the fourth and farthest week back in time. This is usually the best method but you must be flexible and note in the margin of the schedule if the informant starts remembering in an haphazard way. Note which weeks he covers spontaneously and then check on any of the intervening weeks so far not covered to find out whether there were items other than those he has mentioned.

Use open questions, i.e. the type where you ask *"was there or not?"* Guard against using phrases such as *"What was there in week...?"* which suggests you expect there was something. Make use of any Bank Holidays that fall within a memory period. Mention them to your informant, because he may remember whether events fell either side of the holiday in question. If your informant says he cannot remember anything about purchases in the last four weeks ask him to stop and think of the events in this specific period; has he been on holiday or has anything special happened to him in the last four weeks? Once he starts remembering holiday, or family birthdays, he is placing the period and may well find it easy then to go on and remember whether there is any data relevant to your question.

Types of Probe to Avoid

If you need to invent other phrases to use as factual probes take care to avoid the use of any sharp phrases of the kind *"would you be more specific"*. This may be what one is aiming at but precise replies tend to come from thorough but gently worded probes that do not put the informant under duress.

It is necessary for you to avoid the use of **leading** questions. A leading question is one which stresses a certain line or puts an idea into the informant's head. This can be done in both positive and negative ways. Either way is wrong.

An example of a **negative question,** if you wanted to ask an informant to give you an exact reply it would be negative questioning if you said *"you couldn't be more exact about the cost, could you?"* It is a dangerous form of questioning because you are putting the idea into his head that he cannot be exact, whereas you want to encourage him to think and help you by a positive statement, *"could you tell me what the actual (cost) was please?"*

An **inverted question** is one in which instead of openly asking about a topic, e.g. the question *"Do you like cheese or not?"* the interviewer says either *"You do like cheese don't you?"* or *"You don't like cheese do you?"*

There are some interview situations in which it might be perfectly right to resort to leading questions at the instigation of the research officer. It is expected the use of such questions will influence the data, but providing the researcher knows when and what form of stimulus was introduced then allowance can be made for it in analysing the results. It would be dangerous for you to resort to such questioning when not asked to do so, since the research officer could not know of the influence you would have exerted on the replies.

The Legitimacy of D. K. s

An interviewer sometimes feels disappointed or frustrated when she gets large numbers of "Don't know" type answers. Perhaps we all have an urge to get as much information as possible out of other people, but we may be working on survey subjects with relatively low interest levels for some or all sections of the population. It is necessary to remember when probing to stop if it is clear that your informant's mind has gone completely blank on a subject.

81

It is unwise to over-probe even on factual data. If the informant definitely cannot remember, over-probing might drive him to guess, either in order to oblige you or to escape further questioning. The point at which this may begin to happen has to be left to your judgment in the interview. But when you are finding out about purchases or visits over periods of time, once you have established that an item did occur in one of the relevant weeks probe on to see if you can establish the exact day of the week. Do not do this by asking *"was it on (a named) day?"* If the informant says he does not know the day, narrow the field by asking *"can you remember whether it was a week day or a weekend,"* and from this, if a week day, *"was it more likely to be at the beginning, end or middle of a week."* If the actual day has not come to mind by this time record the narrowest range of days concerned.

Difficult interviewing situations do not excuse you from the responsibility of probing adequately, but if the actual circumstances preclude it, as they may if your informant lacks time or shows strong emotional constraint about the topic under enquiry, comment to this effect beside the question. Similarly, if you probe but fail to get data make a note on the schedule about the extent to which you tried.

COMBINATION OF PROBE AND PROMPT

If the research officer knows that a particular question involves a considerable feat of memory on the part of the informant and if, in turn, he knows that the omission in data is likely to be great in consequence, he may design and ask you to use a prompt (i.e. use of suggestion). If he uses this technique on a memory question, most often you will be asked to deal with the question first in an "open" fashion, i.e. to ask the question as it stands; to record the response; to probe fully for all data the informant can spontaneously remember (as specified above). Only **after** the informant has said he cannot think of anything further would you then produce the prompt list. This way the data collected can be analysed as data freely given, against any mentioned after your suggestion. An estimate as to where the true figure lies between the two answers can then be made by the research officer. Combinations of probe and prompt questions are not confined to usage on factual matters. The technique may be used on an opinion survey where we do not want to use forced choice initially (since we are interested in spontaneous replies) but where we do want to compare responses from all informants on a number of points, some of which they would not necessarily volunteer if we left the questioning wholly open.

EXAMPLE 11 OF PROBE AND PROMPT QUESTION ON OPINION SURVEY

(Taken from SS. 333 Labour Mobility)

Q. (a) *"People have to think carefully about a number of things before they decide to move because of a job. What sort of things would you need to be satisfied about before you would go?"*

ring precodes of all mentioned spontaneously in first column. If "good job" use standard probes to find out what informant means by "good job". Also use standard probe "anything else" until informant says "No", then go on to (b) below.	(a) Mentioned spontaneously	(b) if not mentioned spontaneously (Prompt individually)	
		Very important	Not very important
Security of job	1	1	1
Job prospects (pay, promotion)	2	2	2
Good schools	4	4	3
Moving away from friends/Family	10	10	4
Housing	20	20	5
Shopping centres/facilities	40	40	6
Public transport in the area	100	100	7
Social amenities (cinema/theatres/clubs)	200	200	8
Anything else you needed to be satisfied with? (specify)	400		

IF ANY NOT MENTIONED

(b) *"there are other things people have mentioned. Do you think the ones I mentioned are very important or not very important?"*

(individual prompt — for those not mentioned spontaneously — record in (b) above.)

6 Dependent Questions

Main questions on a schedule are meant to be asked of the whole population at whom the survey is directed.

Some questions are meant to be asked only of certain people in the population, or of people who respond in a certain way. This type of question (which may be designed to ascertain facts or opinions) is called a 'dependent' question because its use is dependent on a previously given response or on the type of person being interviewed. During the interview as you record an answer you will need to consider the informant's reply in order to be sure whether the next dependent question is applicable. Dependent questions are usually well sign-posted on the schedule. Opposite, in example 12, a list of places is given. Each place in turn has to be mentioned to the informant (i.e. it is an individual prompt list). The dependent question *"What would be your main reason for not wanting to go (there)?"* is put about each place to which the informant said he would not go.

Note in this example, and in general, if you have a list of items where a dependent question follows, ask the main question in its entirety, i.e. collect primary data first, in this case items 8 to 13 inclusive, before you go on to ask *"Why not"* if they have said *"No"*. This is to stop your informant changing main response in order to avoid the dependent question. This he may do if he is aware that to answer in a certain way results in further questioning of a kind that he finds difficult to answer.

EXAMPLE 12 OF DEPENDENT QUESTION
(Taken from SS. 333 Labour Mobility)

Q. *"Would you move to any of these areas?"*
(Name areas below and show informant on map)

If NO (3), What would be your main reason for not wanting to go (THERE)? (RECORD BELOW)

	D.N.A	YES	NO
South Wales..... (8)	X	2	3
North East England .... (1)	X	2	3
Scotland ....(11)	X	2	3
Northern Ireland ....(13)	X	2	3

I N D I V I D U A L   P R O M P T

DNA = Already lives there

EXAMPLE 13 OF A COMPOSITE QUESTION
(From SS. 386 Reading and Mobility of the Blind)

Q. *"We are interested in the extent to which people get out and about and the amount of walking they do outside. I'd like to ask you about any times you've been out in the past week. Firstly could we talk about the times you went out yesterday. Now yesterday was... (mention day)..."*

USE A SEPARATE JOURNEY LINE FOR TO WORK, AND FROM WORK, AND FOR ANY OTHER OUTING WHICH NATURALLY SPLITS INTO TWO.

START WITH YESTERDAY AND WORK BACKWARDS THROUGH A WEEK. ON ITEM (c) NOTE CODE X IS IN ADDITION TO THE OTHER CODES.

JOURNEY / DAY OF WEEK	(a) What was the main purpose of the journey?					(b) How much time was spent actually travelling	(c) Was it all on foot or did it involve some form of transport. If so, was this a special service for the blind?					(d) How much of the time was on foot?	(e) IF ANY ON FOOT How much was on foot and without a sighted person with you?
	Work	Shopping	Visiting	A walk	Other purpose (specify)	Mins.	All Foot	Car	Bus	Train	Special Service	Mins.	Mins.
1	Y	X	0	1			0	1	2	3	X		
2	Y	X	0	1			0	1	2	3	X		
3	Y	X	0	1			0	1	2	3	X		
4	Y	X	0	1			0	1	2	3	X		
5	Y	X	0	1			0	1	2	3	X		
6	Y	X	0	1			0	1	2	3	X		
7	Y	X	0	1			0	1	2	3	X		
8	Y	X	0	1			0	1	2	3	X		

(spaces for other five days followed on original)

7 Composite Questions

If a series of questions has to be asked about several related things it saves space on the schedule, and facilitates analyses of the results if the questions are arranged as one composite question on the form. (See example 13 on facing page). If we want inventories of purchases, or details of past occupations over a period of time, lists of people living with your informant or lists of day-by-day activities, we often want to know not only how many items (purchases, occupations or activities) are involved but further details about these items. The items are our prime concern and would be called our primary data. The further details we need to have about each item are of importance but are secondary to our knowledge of the existence of the item. The further details would be called the secondary data.

Your **first** aim is to collect the **primary data.** It is more important for us to know that an informant purchased about twenty items or that he has had ten jobs in a period of time, even if he cannot give us minute details about each in turn, than it is to question him fully on each item or job as he mentions it and run the risk of never getting him further back than the last five purchases or four jobs in total.

For this reason on all composite questions remember to collect always the primary data before questioning for secondary data unless told otherwise at the briefing. If an informant knows the extent of your questioning, because you press for secondary, i.e. the descriptive, data before you ask for other main items, consciously or unconsciously he may "forget" the rest because he has become fed up or exhausted by remembering the details.

In example 13 the number of journeys per day would constitute our primary data, but in this example you would find the number of journeys and item (a), on purpose of journeys, would go together since most people remember outings in terms of their purpose. You would take the informant back over the days of the week, working from the most recent day, yesterday through to a week ago to establish all journeys.

Then you would refer to each journey in turn. Once he began to think about a journey you would ask him all the other things, i.e. (b), (c), (d) and (e) about that journey before going on to journey 2, for similar details.

SUMMARY ON HANDLING SUBJECT MATTER

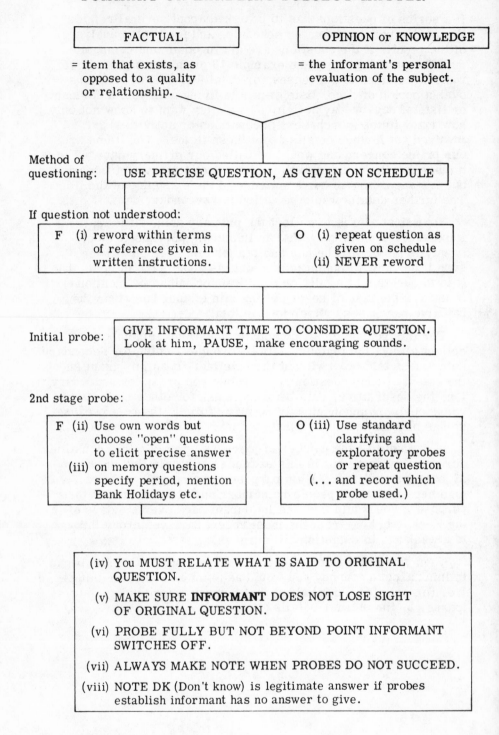

FACTUAL	OPINION or KNOWLEDGE
= item that exists, as opposed to a quality or relationship.	= the informant's personal evaluation of the subject.

Method of questioning: **USE PRECISE QUESTION, AS GIVEN ON SCHEDULE**

If question not understood:

F (i) reword within terms of reference given in written instructions.	O (i) repeat question as given on schedule (ii) NEVER reword

Initial probe: **GIVE INFORMANT TIME TO CONSIDER QUESTION.** Look at him, PAUSE, make encouraging sounds.

2nd stage probe:

F (ii) Use own words but choose "open" questions to elicit precise answer (iii) on memory questions specify period, mention Bank Holidays etc.	O (iii) Use standard clarifying and exploratory probes or repeat question (... and record which probe used.)

(iv) You MUST RELATE WHAT IS SAID TO ORIGINAL QUESTION.

(v) MAKE SURE **INFORMANT** DOES NOT LOSE SIGHT OF ORIGINAL QUESTION.

(vi) PROBE FULLY BUT NOT BEYOND POINT INFORMANT SWITCHES OFF.

(vii) ALWAYS MAKE NOTE WHEN PROBES DO NOT SUCCEED.

(viii) NOTE DK (Don't know) is legitimate answer if probes establish informant has no answer to give.

8 Self-completion

Some studies do involve self-completion; cards, lists, even pictures, for the informant to view may be produced at some stage in the interview. Sometimes the informant is asked to mark items on the cards, in other cases simply to point to codes or sort cards into order. Before field work begins you are told the specific aims of any self-completion items and given specific guidance on the manner in which to handle them.

The first difference between self-completion and the rest of your questioning routine is that for self-completion you must get closer to the informant, possibly at the table if he needs to write. Ensure he has reading glasses on if he uses them. Often you need to read out the items on the card for them to be understood. You will be told at the briefing how much help you can give the informant on any self-completion questions. Revert to your normal interviewing position of sitting face to face, and usually folder on lap, once the self-completion has been dealt with.

Scaling questions have been discussed on pages 66 - 68. In such questions it is easier for you to ask the informant to read and answer for himself such questions which require a degree of agreement or disagreement on ten or twenty items. However, in practice it is only sensible to apply the technique of self-completion with particular populations who are adept at reading and writing.

If we are approaching a population of adolescents, students, teachers or members of professional bodies we may ask them to complete one or more items themselves. **Informants are only to complete items on schedules themselves when the research officer has said they should do so.**

If self-completion forms the main technique to employ on a survey it may be that you will have groups of informants filling in the forms at the same time. Whether or not you have people together, you need to explain what you want done. On educational surveys you may be in a classroom with your group, where you can illustrate the method on the blackboard. Where you are seeing people alone you must point to the appropriate items on the schedule as you hand it to them. Watch carefully to see whether they understand the questions. Be ready to answer any queries.

EXAMPLE 14 OF SPECIAL SELF-COMPLETION (LINEAR) SCALE

(From SS. 352. Deterrents to Crime for Adolescents)

INSTRUCTION TO INTERVIEWER: HAND INFORMANT PENCIL, SHOW INFORMANT THIS PAGE WITH LINES.

Q. *"Now I'd like you to say what chances you think the sort of people who break the law in various ways have of getting away with it. There are some lines here. Each line has 'CERTAIN TO GET CAUGHT' at one end, and 'CERTAIN TO GET AWAY WITH IT' at the other. Will you make a mark on the first line showing what you think the chances are of a person getting away with picking up a wallet containing £100 in the street and keeping it".*

INTERVIEWER: FOR SUBSEQUENT OFFENCES, THERE IS NO NEED TO RUN YOUR FINGER ALONG THE LINE, UNLESS INFORMANT FINDS DIFFICULTY IN FOLLOWING.

	5	15	25	35	45	55	65	75	85	95	
1 Picking up a wallet containing £100 in the street and keeping it. — CERTAIN TO GET CAUGHT											CERTAIN TO GET AWAY WITH IT
2 Breaking into a private house. — CERTAIN TO GET CAUGHT											CERTAIN TO GET AWAY WITH IT
3 Taking an unknown person's car, driving it somewhere 20 miles off and leaving it there. — CERTAIN TO GET CAUGHT											CERTAIN TO GET AWAY WITH IT
4 Stealing things from a large store or supermarket while it is open. — CERTAIN TO GET CAUGHT											CERTAIN TO GET AWAY WITH IT

Linear Scale

On occasions we use a linear representation of a scale for special populations. As in the example opposite you need to explain the purpose of the range of numbers, which is given above the lines, also to draw attention to the statements at either end of each line. Tell the informant that the closer his opinion is to one or other end of the line the nearer to that end of the line he should mark. The numbers above the line are to give him some help in placing his opinion accurately along the line. If this explanation is insufficient you could illustrate the first item by saying

"for example if you thought their chances of getting away and getting caught were equal you would have to mark the centre of the line between 45 and 55, or mark one of the ends if you thought that would happen."

Prompt Cards

If we wish to draw the attention of the informant to a particular
form of question, or series of statements which we want him
to compare, these statements or items will be typed out on
separate cards, called "prompts". Instead of asking an informant
to complete a rating list for himself we might prepare items
for comparison, show him these on sets of cards and ask for
a rank ordering of the items from most to least important.

EXAMPLE 15 OF RANK ORDERING (FROM CARDS)

(From SS. 356.B Home Office. Police/drunkenness.)

INTERVIEWER NOTE: HAND INFORMANT CARDS. ASK QUESTION,
THEN TAKE AWAY EACH CARD IN TURN AS
SUBJECT SELECTS IT.

Q. *"Here are six cards each describing one sort of behaviour. Not
all of them describe offences against the law. Which one of them
would you condemn or disapprove of most if a friend of yours — a
married man of 25 not in the Police — did it?"* (ENTER "1" IN
RANK ORDER COLUMN) *"And which would you condemn or disapprove of least?"* (ENTER "6" IN RANK ORDER COLUMN.)
CONTINUE TILL ALL SIX ARE RANKED.

	RANK
A. Gambling away most of his week's wages (supposing he had no savings to draw on).........	
B. Being drunk and disorderly in the street..........	
C. Going with a prostitute........................	
D. Pilfering material worth £5 from his workplace ...	
E. Deliberately travelling without a ticket on public transport...................................	
F. Failing to declare to the Income Tax Authorities £200 annual income obtained from letting a room in his house or flat.............................	

Method 1 for rank ordering

In rank ordering questions of this kind one has the choice of
two methods for obtaining the ranking. Which method you will
use may have to depend on the number of items to be ranked.
In example 15 you ask the informant to decide on highest and
lowest (condemn/disapprove of most, then least) in turn, then
you ask him for the next highest and lowest of the remainder,
until you are left with a card that represents the middle choice.
This method of ordering is technically the purest since the
informant is asked to think distinctly of opposites, until he
reaches a central point.

Method 2 for rank ordering

If the list is longer than the list given in the example above,
pilot experience may show that informants are muddled by the
above technique. If this were the case you would be told by
the research officer to give the informant all the cards to study.
You would tell the informant that on each card is described a
sort of behaviour. You would explain that you wanted the whole
set ranked from **most** to **least** disapproved of by your informant.
He would then consider all the cards and arrange them as a set
from most to least disapproved of by himself. You would record
the order in which he has arranged them.

By either method if he says he approves or disapproves
equally of two or three of the items then these two or three are
all given the same rank number, but the next ranked card is
numbered to allow for the whole three.

Take our example 15. If an informant ranked A as most (1)
and B as the least (6) followed by F as (2) and then said for the
next least he could not distinguish between D and E, both D and
E would be numbered 5 and the next most serious as 3 ... so
there would be no 4 but two 5s.

Note that the research officer will tell you whether to use
method 1 or 2 or whether you have the choice of method to suit
your informant.

Summary of Points to Observe when Asking Questions

1 **Learn layout of schedule before beginning field work.**

   Learn to scan questions so you are never unsure of sequence and can judge if pace of interview is correct. You need to judge whether you are spending a reasonable proportion of time on any one question according to its relative importance to the subject of the survey.

2 **Ask the questions in sequence and in the exact words in which they are printed on the schedule** in the first instance, and use a conversational but deliberate tone so that the informant has the best chance of hearing the question. Guard against any lapse into your own words and listen carefully to your informant throughout.

3 **Watch out for people mishearing or misunderstanding questions.** A likely source of error is that they are still thinking about the answer they have given to a previous question. It is not necessary for them to ask you to repeat a question again before you may do so. Remember the informant will not know and cannot be expected to know survey definitions. It is your task to decide how to classify the facts and not the informant's.

4 **Use preambles or linking comments when passing from one group of questions to the next in order to prepare the** informant for the change of subject.

5 **Use only standard probes on opinion questions but use them fully.** Remember they are only effective if used efficiently; think whether the need is for more or for clarifying data when deciding which probe to use. Always bear the question fully in mind when you are deciding whether to probe further.

6 **On probing for facts constantly watch that familiarity with a schedule and with similar kinds of replies does not lead you into the habit of half assuming responses.** The use of inverted and leading questions is a sign that this may be happening.

7 **Do not read back to informants what they have said to you** unless you must quote back one or two words in order to show them what you want to know more about.

8 **If you need to repeat a question** or if you consider that the informant has misunderstood, **generally adopt the line that you may have failed to make something clear** which is why you want to go back over it.

Chapter 10

RECORDING

MANNER OF RECORDING DATA

It is important for us to have precise answers and correct representation of views from informants whenever possible, since each informant represents a large number of people in the population and any error in an interview represents a large error in total.

In chapter 9 we have discussed the types of question used to convey meaning to informants. Our next consideration is how you will record data.

Accuracy in recording is essential. Your informants' answers must be RECORDED AT THE TIME OF INTERVIEW. You need to be familiar with the different ways of recording responses in order to record satisfactorily without holding up the flow of the interview.

A. PRECODED RECORDING

Precoding is a device for recording answers speedily, and for facilitating the ultimate sorting out and counting of the information collected. Whenever all the possible answers to a question can be foreseen, these answers are listed on the recording schedule and numbered, so that the interviewer has merely to put a ring round the appropriate number at the time of interview.

There are two potential sources of error on precoded answers:

1 Careless ringing of the wrong code. Prior study of the schedule so that you know exactly where codes lie on the form can help to overcome this type of error.

2 Misrepresentation of the informant's reply. This can happen if you are unaware of the instructions on what to include in which category, or it can happen if you believe you are sure to get only answers which fall within the categories given on the form. If you believe this then you may hear incorrectly, or fail to probe with sufficient care on ambiguous replies.

In example 17 there is an open "other answer specify" 4, beside which you record any answer given which does not fit precisely into any of the other categories.

If you put the question (example 17) to an informant and she says

"yes the children"

you will be unable to code this answer because it is not clear what she means. You could not jump to the conclusion it must fit precode 1 because she has mentioned the word 'children' which occurs in that code. You would need to say *"can you explain a little more fully what you mean?"*

She may then go on to say:

"Yes I mean I am worried by the number of children in the class, there are too many per class for my child to be well taught"

In which case her answer will fit into code 3. But this you could not have guessed from the first statement. It is often necessary to use the clarifying probe in this way to decide the meaning of a response.

The "other specify" code will be used to cover items that we had not thought of in our list and for qualified answers of the kind where a person starts off by saying *"I cannot generalise, it depends"*, and goes on to tell you all his qualifications.

From this you will see that precoding saves a little time for the interviewer. Sometimes a given answer immediately fits into one of the groups and you can ring the code without writing out what is being said, but in many cases it is only after probing that you find out which code, if any, is applicable. In such cases you will have started writing down the answer, whilst you were sorting out what was meant. If, subsequently, it fits into a precode, cross through the verbatim which you have coded into a category.

Everything the informant has already said on a given topic or your knowledge of other informants' answers, may lead you to expect the informant to answer a certain question in a particular way, and this almost unconscious expectation may cause you to mishear, or misinterpret, the informant's answer unless you listen most intently to get the exact meaning of what is being said.

EXAMPLE 16 OF PRECODING

(From SS.379 Womens Employment)

Q. *"On what would you say the money you earn is mostly spent?"*

	Code
Contributions to housekeeping including rent	1
Clothes for self........................	2
Clothes for children	3
Buying household appliances	4
Holidays	5
Saving to buy a house	6
Running/buying a car (for self or family)..	7
Children's education....................	8
Saving for own old age	9
Saving for marriage	X
Other savings..........................	Y
Other things ....SPECIFY	O

DO NOT PROMPT. CODE ALL THAT APPLY.

EXAMPLE 17 OF PRECODED REPLIES

(From SS.365 Survey of Parents of Primary School Children)

Q. *"Is there anything which you are not happy about or which worries you about (CHILD'S PRESENT SCHOOL) which you haven't already mentioned?"*

	Code
Other children rough, bullying; badly hehaved/spoken	1
Bad, old fashioned buildings, lack of facilities, poor equipment	2
Too large classes, shortage of teachers	3
Other (specify below)	4

It can be difficult to determine the category of an informant's response because:

(i) he may say one thing spontaneously and then go on to contradict himself.

(ii) he may use words which occur in the precode but conceptually his whole answer means something other than the meaning of the precode category.

(iii) contrarily, he may be giving a reply in the exact terms of reference of the precode without using the form of words we have chosen for it.

You must satisfy yourself that the concept of the precode selected covers precisely the concept of the informant's reply

For example, if we had given you a precode for:

Don't know (D.K.).......... 1

If a person said *"I don't know (pause) perhaps it's a good idea"*

Following from point (i) (above) you would need to repeat the question to see whether this meant he did not know or whether he definitely thought it a good idea.

If the person said *"don't know how to put it in words but I do feel very strongly that it is a good idea"* (under point (ii) above) you do **not** code "D.K." just because he happened to use the words of our precode. He used them in a different context from the one in which we had used them, ending by stating positive favour for the idea.

If the person looked at you blankly and said, in answer to your question, *"I haven't got a clue"* (point (iii) above you would code "D.K."..........1 without further question. He is the only person out of the three who is answering to the effect that he really does not know, and you do not need to get him to mouth the actual words of the precode before coding "D.K."

When precoding replies you must always make sure that you have correctly heard and understood the informant's reply and must at all times guard against letting personal opinions influence judgment.

The precoded categories are arrived at by Coding Branch from their study of the most frequent types of response that occurred on the pilot (trial) study. Most often they leave one open category beside which you can give details of any type reply that does not fit into the other given groups. It is best to put the answer under "Others" and give a verbatim record of the informant's answer, if there is **any** doubt whether it fits into one of the precodes, so that it can be considered afterwards. On the other hand remember that you are in the best position to have responses clarified. In the field, with the informant, you can ask him to *"explain (any answer)"*; this cannot be done once the interview is over.

B. OPEN RECORDING

In cases where no precoding is provided it is important to write in fully the given answer to a question. Replies in the form of a figure, that is to say an age, a date or an amount of money are required in exact amounts. If all efforts to get an actual amount fail then an "e" for estimate or approximate is to be recorded beside the amount given.

Coders have the task of devising a coding frame from "open" responses. They have to count the number of different replies occurring in answer to a question and note the range of replies in order to decide with the research officer the content and number of categories to use per question. It is only possible to arrive at satisfactory categories if you have recorded given answers in enough detail for us not to be in doubt as to what the answers mean.

Open recording mostly follows from open questions (see chapter 9 page 63). This is because an open question often produces a long, complicated response which would be difficult for you to sort out into categories at the time of interview.

Open Responses are to be recorded longhand and verbatim:

(i) **Word for word**

(ii) **in the first person/exactly as the informant states his ideas on each question**

(iii) **at the time of interview.**

Digressions by the informant can be omitted if they are clearly irrelevant to the question-objectives, but responses are so rarely clearly irrelevant that mostly all that is said needs to be recorded. Sometimes an informant seems to ramble off the point but is actually giving useful information in terms of his interpretation of the question. We try to leave enough space on a schedule for the average verbatim answer to be recorded fully. If the space provided is insufficient, take the rest down in the margin of the schedule, i.e. always on the same page, and arrow the answer firmly to the relevant question.

The only way to achieve verbatim recording is to start writing immediately the informant starts to talk. Avoid summarising any reply, but if you meet a most garrulous person and cannot record every word then you must be sure to include all concepts and telling phrases from the reply. Words abbreviated at the time of interview will have to be written over in full by you before returning the schedule to Headquarters. **Never rewrite the whole schedule, always return the original used in the field.**

Practice verbatim recording regularly and certainly before a survey if you have not used verbatim for a few months. Remember persons not present at the interview will be coding and tabulating the data, and therefore they can code only on what words are recorded on the schedule. An answer left with vague abbreviations or unclear sentence shortenings could result in the response being unusable. You have the benefit of seeing the informant's facial expression and hearing the tone of voice accompanying an answer. The coders will have only the written word. Therefore if there is anything peculiar in the informant's manner or expression whilst he is giving a reply, which is not reflected in the words, e.g. a person answering tongue in cheek *"Oh yes I've got a Rolls Royce and a Daimler"* you should add a note about the informant's demeanour and thereby the meaning of his words.

The coders can only devise a coding frame from open responses if you have probed answers fully and recorded all that has been said. **In response to questions not of fact but of opinion the informant's own words should be recorded because the way in which he expresses himself may affect the category into which his reply would come.** If, however, he expresses himself in dialect, uses initials or includes any words that either have two meanings or are words not in general use, you need to ask for an explanation of these words at the time of recording them. Enter both the original and explanatory words. Never accept an unclear word without query nor substitute what you think it means. You can easily miss out data, leaving apparent inconsistent or ambiguous replies, even when you do report the informant word for word. This is because what he says is often clear because of the context in which it is said. If you relate the written word too closely to your remembrance of the interview when checking it, you may remember the informant's facial expression and previous comments too well and use them to colour the words and clarify them in your own mind, and fail to see that what is written remains unclear.

After the interview allow an hour or so to elapse before you check a schedule in order to overcome the above problem, but never leave your checking longer than one day, or you will have forgotten too much about the interview. Help coders by adding, in parentheses, any notes relating to the informant's facial expression etc. which will add to what has been written in answer to the questions.

100

Indicating probes on schedules

Similarly, to help coders who do not have the advantage of sitting in on the interview it is helpful to them if you indicate where you have probed open replies. It is enough to make a diagonal mark as you use the probe; and indicate by the use of initials which probe was used:

"/ae" = "Is there anything else?"
"are there any other (reasons)?" – if appropriate

"/exp" = "can you explain that a little more fully?"

"/way" = "in what way?"

"/how" = "how do you mean?"

Whenever you have to repeat the question by way of probe indicate this on the schedule as:

"/R" = repeat.

If a probe is used and produces nothing it is useful to us if you indicate this.

"/____"

However, in any stress situation, it is more important that you remember to use the right probe than that you find time to write it in. Certainly do both if you can do so without slowing up the natural speed at which your informant is talking and you are reporting his words.

Special Instructions on precoded questions

Beside a precoded question on a schedule you may be told in print to

CODE ONE ONLY

or

CODE ALL THAT APPLY

These instructions must be carefully observed and if you study the question for which either instruction is given, the point of allowing only one or many codes is usually apparent as in the cases opposite where in Example 18 we do not wish to confine the informant to any one aspect of schooling but ask her openly to say any or many things she has in mind about her child's school and schooling in general.

Whenever you have an instruction to "CODE ALL THAT APPLY" note that it cannot mean you can code two mutually contradictory answers to the same question, e.g. in example 18 you could not have any of the codes 1 to 6 ringed if under code 7 you had

written down *"I have no criticism whatsoever of that school. I think it is excellent in teaching method and suits Brian very well".*

In Example 19, though the preamble to the question says doctors are interested in heating of rooms, the actual question asks in which one room does the informant spend most of the day.

In Example 19, if the informant mentions two types of room, e.g. *"Oh in the kitchen else the living room,"* since we ask for one only you must refer the informant back to the question by repeating it. *"Well in which room (would you say) you spend most of the day/time when you are at home?"*

EXAMPLE 18 OF MULTI-CODING OR "ALL THAT APPLY"

(From SS.365 Parents of Primary School Children)

Q. *"Is there anything else that you would like to say about...*
(child's name)...school, or about infants or junior
schooling in general?"

		Code
	Criticisms of large classes, overcrowding, shortage of teachers	1
	Criticisms of school buildings, accommodation, facilities, equipment......................	2
CODE ALL THAT APPLY.	Criticisms of school meals; food or drink provided at breaks	3
	Children should be segregated by sex in infants/junior schools.....................	4
	In infants/juniors, problem or unfairness of starting or changing schools by month of birthday (e.g. have to stay extra year or have year less in infants/juniors)	5
	Criticisms of 11 as age of transfer to/ selection for secondary school	6
	Other (specify)	7

EXAMPLE 19 OF ONE CODE ONLY

(From SS.366 Social Welfare for the Elderly)

"Doctors are very interested in heating of rooms — so
I'd like to ask you about heating arrangements in the
room you use most."

Q. *"In which room do you spend most of the day/time*
when you're at home?"

		Code
	Living room	1
CODE ONE ONLY.	Bedsitter	2
	Bedroom	3
	Kitchen	4

EXAMPLE 20 OF PRECODES – "OPEN-ENDED"

(From SS.389 Schools Council Early Leavers)

Q. *"When the time to think about the choice of job (or career) for a child comes along a lot of parents wonder what to do about it."* They can either

(READ OUT)

	... Make the choice for the youngster and tell him that is what he's got to do	1
CODE ONE ONLY	OR Discuss possible jobs with him and let him make a choice	2
	OR Not say anything and allow him to make up his own mind	3

.... Which of these will (did) you do in *(child's name)* ....'s case, or will (did) you do something different? I will read them out again".

(READ OUT ABOVE LIST AGAIN).

(unprompted)	Not thought about it yet, youngster too young yet	4
	Will do (did) something else ..SPECIFY	5

PRECODED, OPEN-ENDED RECORDING

It has been mentioned that it is common to have an amalgam of method, (A) and (B) namely a set of precoded responses which are "open-ended", i.e. having a final "other answer specify" for use where the answers given do not fall within the concepts covered in the precoded items. Such an "other answer" is then to be treated by you as an "open" response and must be written up fully in the manner explained page 99. Once it reaches the office coders have to look at the content of the "other" code and devise new categories according to the number of fresh concepts mentioned.

Dependent questions

(See Chapter 9, on usage). Sometimes you are given a code to ring beside any dependent question when it does not apply in an interview. This is to help you handle the schedule methodically by knowing you must ring a code or write an answer at the time of interview to **every** question on the form. It would be shown as follows:

D. N. A. (Does not apply) 1

If no such code is provided rule a pencilled diagonal line through the question and answer space.

EXAMPLE 21 of layout of DEPENDENT question without a D. N. A.

(From SS. 372 Housing Survey)

Q. *"Have you a built-in cupboard or larder for storing food?"*

	Code
Yes	Y
No	X

IF YES (Y)

(a) *"Is it ventilated — that is, can the outside air get to it?"*

Yes	0
No	1

EXAMPLE 22 OF BOX LAYOUT

(From SS.329 Motoring Survey)

Q. *"Have you been away on holiday with the car in the last 12 months?"* .... No. 0
(HOLIDAY HERE MEANS AN ABSENCE WITH THE CAR OF A WEEK OR MORE)   Yes 1

    IF YES (1) *"How many times?"* .... Number ....

IF ONE OR MORE HOLIDAYS (Code 1)

	Holiday 1		Holiday 2		Holiday 3	
	Month	Wks.	Month	Wks.	Month	Wks.
(a) How many weeks were you away with the car and during which months? GIVE WEEKS SEPARATELY FOR EACH MONTH OR GIVE DATES	....	....	....	....	....	....
(b) About how many miles did your holiday motoring in this car amount to?	Miles		Miles		Miles	
(c) Was any of this motoring done outside England and Wales?	Yes .... 1 No. 2		Yes .... 1 No. 2		Yes .... 1 No. 2	
IF YES (1) (i) How much?	Miles		Miles		Miles	
(ii) In what countries?						
(d) How many people were in the car, including the driver, when most of the mileage was done?	Number		Number		Number	

Box layout

It follows from the use of composite questions (see Chapter 9 on usage) that some box layout is provided on the schedule for recording replies. The questions to be asked may be written out in full above the box or you may be given only key words there. If the latter then you must study well the definition of each question as given you in the survey's instructions in order to know the right questions to pose.

Self-completion forms:

(See Chapter 9, for usage). Self-completion forms are filled in by the informant at the time of interview and so the interviewer should have no work on these forms other than

(i)   to add any necessary serial number and append them to the parent schedule in whatever manner instructed at the briefing.

(ii) to check that an answer is in fact recorded to each relevant question. This must be done in the informant's presence. After taking the form back from the informant write in the margin any doubts you have about the way in which the form has been completed and note any comments he has made about his interpretation of some of the items.

Prompt cards

(See Chapter 9, for usage). Prompt cards are provided for each survey on which they are required. A prompt card for income details is provided on most surveys, but the suggested groupings vary from survey to survey. Therefore you must take care to check that you have the right card bearing numbers corresponding to the sums of money that occur on your schedule. Watch out for informants' misuse of categories if you want to avoid ringing a wrong code. In particular watch that the old age pensioner or housewife with a small income who quotes *"well its none because it is not up to number 1"* in fact gets coded group 1 (if group 1 is meant to cover "up to £5") and not 0 (nil) as she is suggesting.

Take care to have a good supply of prompt cards and have them to hand during the interview so that you can pass them to the informant at the time of putting the appropriate question without any hold-up in your questioning.

Summary of Points to observe in recording

1 **There must be a response recorded in every applicable answer space on the schedule.**

   Unless a response or a NIL or a line is drawn through the answer column to a question the coders have to assume that question was not put to the informant.

2 **Always use pencil for completing schedules.**

3 **All answers must be recorded at the time of interview.**
   Any words or notes added after the interview must be clearly marked as such, since the accuracy of words remembered will differ from accuracy of the same taken down in situ.

4 Cross out rather than rub out wrong recording. **Use one diagonal line to cross out wrong figures** (a cross can be mistaken for a coded X).

5 **Study the scope of the precodes and do not jump to the conclusion that a half-given answer fits.** On the other hand do not be so unsure of yourself that you force the informant to mouth the actual words of the precode before you will classify his answer.

6 **Make sure any part of a verbatim reply you subsequently decide can be put into a precode is firmly crossed out** so that coders do not ponder on whether it is meant to be an "other specify" answer.

7 **Never write across "office use only" columns.** These "tramlines" at the right hand side and sometimes centre of a page are computers' columns in which one is allowed to ring code numbers but not to write in verbatim replies.

8 Always give full explanatory notes of odd circumstances affecting any given answer. **Put necessary notes, in parentheses, somewhere on the same page as the item to which they refer.** Clearly arrow these to the appropriate question. Do not pin notes on the schedule as they can easily get torn off.

9 **Make a note beside any question where, in error, you deviated from question wording or the required degree of probing,** i.e. note why and to what extent you deviated, so that allowance can be made for it, if necessary, when data is being coded.

10 **Remember to add an identifying serial number or mark to each schedule at the time of interview** to avoid confusing one schedule with another.

11 **Mark any question "omitted in error" as such.** If the matter is factual and the probable or estimated answer is known to you, record this fact beside your admittance of omission in any case where your quota is finished. But if you are still working in the area go back to the house to put the matter right. If the omission is of an opinion question neither go back to the house for data nor attempt any estimated reply but record as above beside the question "omitted to ask in error".

12 **Remember to show "e" for estimate beside any figure which you know is not an exact figure.**

13 **Above all check the schedule after interview for LEGIBILITY and leave as allowable abbreviations only:**

DNA = does not apply

DK	= don't know	gvt	= government	w'd	= would
eg	= example	∴	= therefore	sh'd	= should
&	= and	∵	= because	c'd	= could

14 Although no actual space is provided on the schedule for it do tell us of interviewer difficulties. If your probing was unsuccessful, in part or throughout, say so. We need to know the value of interviews and to know in retrospect which questions, if any, were least successful and for what reason.

Chapter 11

THE CLASSIFICATION SECTION

At each interview some facts are required which will describe the person interviewed. By collecting such facts as sex, age, and occupation we are then able to say what kinds of people our survey represents. We can also discover how the opinions and attitudes expressed by the informants and the facts they give about themselves vary according to the sort of person giving the information. For example, by looking at the answers given by men and women of different social groups, family size or ages we can see in what ways, if any, their responses differ according to these factors.

Points (1) to (12) below cover the background information which we seek most often from an informant.

(1)   Age and sex.

(2)   Type of Household.

(3)   Head of Household.

(4)   Housewife.

(5)   Marital Status.

(6)   Whether working or not.

(7)   Occupation and Industry.

(8)   Income.

(9)   Type of dwelling.

(10) No: of Rooms in dwelling.

(11) Type of Education.

(12) Educational Qualifications.

In order to standardise the information we collect and to enable comparisons to be made between the way sections of the community respond on one survey subject and another, the Government Social Survey has evolved a number of definitions of the above twelve classification items.

Unless specific instructions are given to the contrary the definitions of these twelve items (as given below) always apply. It is vitally important that you should apply them correctly so that the research officer, when he comes to make his report, knows precisely what is included in each of the categories.

Item 1. AGE AND SEX

We need to know the age and sex of your informant and, in many surveys, the ages and sex of the persons with whom he resides. This necessitates you asking the sex of any persons not present at the interview in any cases where the way in which the informant refers to them leaves you in some doubt, e. g. *"a friend"*.

For age a precise figure is required.

To get an exact answer you must ask for age in the form of

"age last birthday".

Without the use of this definition throughout, elderly people and young children's ages would invariably be given inaccurately.

Item 2. TYPE OF HOUSEHOLD

We need to lay down rules as to which people should be included as members of any household to avoid the risk of counting twice or omitting any member of the public at a given residence. Before you do ask for ages and any other data make sure you have found out the total number of people to be included, as regular members of the informant's household, according to the following definition.

Item 2. A HOUSEHOLD

A household is a group of people who all live regularly at the address given on the sample list, and who are all catered for, for at least one meal a day, by the same person.

Any other individual or group of individuals in the same dwelling who has different catering arrangements forms a separate household.

POINTS TO REMEMBER

The two important facts to be established are:

1. **that all persons in a household are catered for by the same person.**

   BEING CATERED FOR is defined as:

   (a) **having at least one meal a day, when in residence.**

2. **that all persons live there regularly.**

   LIVING THERE REGULARLY means:

   (b) for relatives and other persons, they are included if they spend **at least 4 nights a week** in this household — even if they are regularly away from it for the remaining 3 or less nights. It is four nights every week which counts for household membership and not an average of four nights per week over a period of time.

   (c) for married persons, they are included if they do return to their spouse at this household at **least one night a week.** This covers spouses who work away from home and can only return home week-ends.

Clearly you will meet cases which the above criterion does not satisfy. You must know what to do with other people who are mentioned as absentees or visitors. You must decide from the following whether or not to include them.

In addition to people who satisfy conditions (a) and (b) or (a) and (c) you must count as members, i.e.

INCLUDE IN THE HOUSEHOLD:

(d) People on holiday, away on a rare business trip or in hospital at time of interview. who normally live in the household (satisfying points (a) and (b) or (a) and (c)), unless they have been away for more than six months (if it is precisely 6 months on the day of interview, include them).

(e) Fishermen and any merchant seamen whose only shore address this is and who normally spend up to and including, but not more than, six weeks at sea.

(f) Children under 16 away at boarding or other schools. (This is an exception to Point (g) below).

You do not count people solely on the basis that the informant considers this to be their home address. You will therefore

EXCLUDE FROM THE HOUSEHOLD:

(g) Members of the family of 16 years and over who live away from home and who only come home for holidays (this will cover persons away at school, or college, as well as those working away from home).

(h) Members of the Forces (and Merchant Navy) stationed permanently away from home. (Of course, if they were stationed permanently at home then they would be included in the household.)

(i) Temporary members of the household. Relatives who do not normally live there, and persons home on leave from abroad etc. They would only be included in the household if they had been there for **more than six months** prior to the date of interview.

(NOTE: This six months' rule applies only to temporary members of the household. Anyone who has joined the household within the last six months as a regular member, that is someone with no intention of leaving the household, is no longer considered a temporary member of the household).

When asking for **HOUSEHOLD** Composition, it is simplest to ask:

"How many people live here regularly, who are catered for by the same person as yourself?"

Both the concepts of residence and having meals must be mentioned. Even with the use of this exact question further probing may be necessary when the informant says, for example, she has boarders or relatives staying there.

Never confuse our definition of the terms boarder and lodger.

(i)   **Boarders.** These are members of the household, who are not related by blood or marriage to any other members of the household. They receive accommodation for at least four nights a week, and, when they are in residence, at least one meal per day from the house-wife, in return for payment. These are called "boarders". So that our definitions are consistent, they are included in the landlord's household **unless** they are married and return home to their spouse at least one night every week. (See Point (c) page 112 by which we would be counting them, theoretically, in a household elsewhere.)

(ii)   **Lodgers.** By a lodger we mean someone who caters for himself and is therefore not a member of this household because he forms a separate household.

You will see from the above that we are establishing the number of people living in private households.

NOTE:

(iii) A household can consist of only one person.

(iv)   Members of the household need not be related by blood or marriage.

If you follow the above definition you will have excluded those persons who form the floating population by living in hotels, hostels or are of no fixed abode. If your informant is the pro-prietor or belongs to the proprietor's household of an hotel or commercial boarding house or hostel, the guests are not included in the proprietor's (i.e. informant's) household. We define a commercial boarding house as one which caters for AT LEAST FOUR BOARDERS at the time of interview. In smaller establish-ments (i.e. any household with three or less boarders) the boarders are included in the landlord's household.

Establishing persons with specific roles in a household

In EXAMPLE 23 of HOUSEHOLD BOX LAYOUT you will see that we need to establish the informant's position in the household; to find out whether he holds a key position 'Head of that Household' (being the figure from whom we determine the household's social class) or if not to see his relationship to whoever is the Head of Household and the housewife.

EXAMPLE 23 OF LAYOUT FOR HOUSEHOLD BOX

	Relationship to Subject	Sex		AGE
	(Ref: Item 2)	M	F	(Ref: Item 1)
A	SUBJECT	1	2	
B		1	2	
C		1	2	
D		1	2	
E		1	2	
F		1	2	
G		1	2	

HOH is person (give letter) ....

H/W is person (give letter) ....

Note on this example you are asked to record members in relationship to SJT. (sometimes called informant). On page 13 is an example of a household box where relationship required is to H.O.H.

(The definitions of H.O.H. and H/W. follow in items 3 and 4)

CRITERION OF HOUSEHOLD MEMBERSHIP

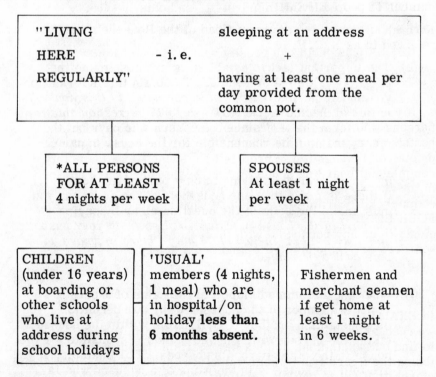

"LIVING HERE REGULARLY" - i.e. sleeping at an address + having at least one meal per day provided from the common pot.

*ALL PERSONS FOR AT LEAST 4 nights per week

SPOUSES At least 1 night per week

CHILDREN (under 16 years) at boarding or other schools who live at address during school holidays

'USUAL' members (4 nights, 1 meal) who are in hospital /on holiday **less than 6 months absent.**

Fishermen and merchant seamen if get home at least 1 night in 6 weeks.

*Unless a BOARDER who goes home to spouse 1 night per week.

It is important to establish the household composition before establishing who to regard as the Head of Household or Housewife, because who **can** be regarded as H.O.H. or H/W is governed by the household composition.

(i)   In each household there can be only one Head of Household and one Housewife.

(ii)   Though the Head of the Household (H.O.H.) and the housewife (H/W) can be one and the same person.

Item 3.   HEAD OF HOUSEHOLD (H.O.H.)

The Head of the Household must be a member of the household (by our definition). The Head of the Household is, in order of precedence, the husband of the person, or the person who either:

(a) Owns the household accommodation.

(b) Is legally responsible for the rent or the accommodation.

(c) Has the household accommodation as an emolument or perquisite.

(d) Has the household accommodation by virtue of some relationship to the owner in cases where the owner or lessee is not a member of the household.

POINTS TO REMEMBER

Throughout schedules the term Head of the Household will be referred to as H.O.H.

(e) The important fact to establish is in whose name the property is owned or rented. To obtain this information you should normally ask *"In whose name is this house/flat owned or rented"*. Do **NOT** ask *"Who is responsible for PAYING the rent?"* since the person who pays out the money may not be responsible for the house **in name.**

If your informant is living in only part of the house, i.e. if there is more than one household at the address, you must make the point of the question clear by saying *"For the part of the house in which you live (with your husband and your mother-in-law etc.) may I know in whose name it is owned or rented?"*

(f) When the accommodation is in the name of a person who is not a member of the household (by our definition), you must establish another H.O.H. from within the household, taking the person within it who stands responsible for the house in the other person's absence. For example, if you are told the house is in the name of a husband who is stationed away from home, he is not a member of the household, and in this case you can take as the H.O.H. his wife who is living there.

(g) So long as the husband is resident he takes precedence over the wife in being H.O.H. This means if you have a married couple living together, even if the wife owns the property or has her name on the rent book, you count her husband as the H.O.H.

Where the household consists only of mother, father and children under 21 years, no questions as to who is the H.O.H. need be asked since, by the above rule, you take the father as the H.O.H. In all cases where there is any other adult (except boarders) living in the household you must ask " *in whose name etc.* " since the house could be in the name of one of the other adults.

(h) When two persons of different sex have an equal claim to be H.O.H., i.e. if you are told ownership is joint, then you take the male of the two to be the H.O.H.

(i) When two persons of the same sex have equal claim to be H.O.H., i.e. if you are told ownership is joint, then you take the elder of the two as H.O.H.

Item 4. HOUSEWIFE (H/W)

The housewife is the person, other than a domestic servant, who is responsible for most of the domestic duties.

(a) If these tasks are done by a paid servant, the servant is not the housewife. In such a case the housewife is the person responsible for seeing that the servant performs these tasks.

POINTS TO REMEMBER

(b) The important fact is who is responsible for MOST of the domestic duties in the household.

When asking for **HOUSEWIFE** never single out separate items such as cleaning or cooking, else the point of the definition is lost. Ask:

"Who is mainly responsible for the domestic duties?"

or, for a multi-household:

"Which of you is responsible for the domestic duties in this part of the house?"

The informant must be allowed to interpret *"most of the domestic duties"* for himself.

117

ESTABLISHING PERSONS WITH SPECIFIC
ROLES IN A HOUSEHOLD

A HOUSEHOLD (H/hd)

A group of people living
here regularly and being
catered for by same person.
It must contain person(s)
with roles of:

HEAD of HOUSEHOLD (H.O.H.)

the person (resident) in
whose name the premise/
(accommodation occupied by
H/hd) is owned or rented

HOUSEWIFE (H/W)

the person mainly
responsible for most of
the domestic duties
(unspecified)

If two people (residents) of opposite sex, have equal claim to be

H.O.H.   or   H/W

(take) male of the two   (take) female of the two

If two people (resident) of the same sex have equal claim

(take) elder   (take) elder

Special considerations

If told person "in whose
name" is **not** a member of
H/hd count as H.O.H. person
in H/hd who takes
responsibility for absentee.

Paid servant cannot be
H/W. H/W is resident
person to whom servant
is responsible.

(c) If two persons of different sex share the housekeeping duties EQUALLY then the woman is the housewife, though a man CAN be the housewife if he carries out MOST of the domestic duties, or is responsible for seeing that a paid servant does so. Where the household consists only of mother, father and children under 21 years, by the above rule, the mother is the H/W. In all cases where there is any other adult (except boarders) living in the household you must ask the question.

(d) If two persons of the same sex have equal claim to be the housewife then the elder of the two is the housewife.

Item 5. MARITAL STATUS

We sometimes need to know whether members of the household are married, widowed or single. Divorced persons and those separated from their spouses are coded as widowed. There is no need to ask whether people are divorced or separated, this information will only be collected if it is volunteered.

When asking for **MARITAL STATUS** it is necessary to mention all the alternatives included on the schedule. This should be done in the form of a running prompt, i.e.

"Are you married, single or widowed?"

An example of coding layout for this question follows, where, as is usual, it is incorporated in household box. (Example 24 overleaf).

This example of household box layout contains as many categories as occur on most surveys.

119

EXAMPLE 24 OF HOUSEHOLD BOX LAYOUT

Per: No.	Relation-ship to H.O.H.	OFF; USE	Sex		Age last birth-day	Marital Status (Ref. item 5)			Working Status (Ref. item 6)		
			M	F		M	S	W	Full-time	Part-time	Not work-ing
1	H.O.H.		1	2		1	2	3	1	2	3
2			1	2		1	2	3	1	2	3
3			1	2		1	2	3	1	2	3
4			1	2		1	2	3	1	2	3
5			1	2		1	2	3	1	2	3
6			1	2		1	2	3	1	2	3
7			1	2		1	2	3	1	2	3
8			1	2		1	2	3	1	2	3
9			1	2		1	2	3	1	2	3
10			1	2		1	2	3	1	2	3

Item 6. WORK AND EMPLOYMENT INFORMATION

In most surveys we need to establish whether members of the household are working or not. (See right hand column of example 24).

WORKING

By working we mean gainful, that is to say paid employment. Gainful employment results either in

(i)   Wages or salary in return for working for an employer for more than ten hours a week at the time of interview. (Anyone working for ten hours or less a week is counted as not working.)

(ii)   Income, as a result of being self-employed for more than ten hours a week. A self-employed person is one whose main responsibility for his work is to himself.

A distinction is drawn between those people who are not working (i. e. retired people, housewives, full-time students) and those who are unemployed.

UNEMPLOYED is defined as not falling into categories (i) and (ii) above, but, actively seeking work. One can actively seek work by registering at a Labour Exchange or other employment agency, or by answering advertisements or advertising for jobs.

NOT WORKING

A person who is not employed and does not intend to apply for work is counted as not working.

CODING

In Example 24 (right hand column) you will note codes occur for Full, Part-time and Not working. In order to code a person who is **gainfully employed** (i. e. in paid work) either Full or Part-time you must establish whether he works as follows:

FULL time is **over 30 hrs** per week

PART time is **over 10 hrs** per week and up to and **including** 30 hrs.

For persons receiving full-time education, i. e. children and students, code (3) not working, and disregard any part-time (vacation and paper round) jobs which they may have.

Note that any person serving an apprenticeship who may be receiving part-time education (day release or sandwich course) is to be coded WORKING (1) if he is paid a wage for his apprenticeship.

The LENGTH OF THE WORKING WEEK (over thirty hours or over ten and up to and including thirty hours) is decided on the number of hours as follows:

(a) A basic working week agreed between the employer and the employee.

(b) The usual working week for a self-employed person.

(c) The number of hours worked in the seven days prior to the day of interview for a casual worker (a fee paid interviewer would be regarded as casual worker for our purposes).

(d) If a person has two or more jobs, the foregoing criteria about hours should be applied to each job. The total number of hours spent on all the jobs should be taken as the length of that person's working week.

(e) A person on holiday or on strike, or not actually employed for any reason beyond his control whilst under agreement to work counts as working.

(f) Persons on sick leave who have a job kept open for them, and to which they can return when they have recovered, would be coded as working full-time or part-time according to which category they are in when fit.

(g) An unemployed person, i.e. one who is actively seeking work, is coded as working full or part-time according to which he was in his last job. This applies on all surveys where no separate code is given for unemployed.

THE NOT WORKING code is used, not only for persons who have no gainful employment and are not seeking any, but also for those

(i) persons who work only up to and including 10 hrs per week.

(ii) any person who says he is sick but has to seek a new job or re-employment with his former firm (not simply return to job kept open for him) when he recovers.

When asking whether the informant is **WORKING** or not it is necessary to explain our definition of working:

"Are you in paid employment at present?"

if the answer is "yes" then ask:

"Is that full-time, i.e. over 30 hours a week or not?"

If not ask:

"Is it part-time, i.e. over 10 and up to and including 30 hours?

Remember that it is paid employment that we are interested in, and only current employment is to be included. It is incorrect to ask only *"Are you working?"* since housewives consider they work in the home and voluntary workers may consider they work for charities.

Item 7. OCCUPATION AND INDUSTRY

Often we want to have details of the informant's occupation and
the industry, trade or profession with which he is associated.
Sometimes we also want similar data for the Head of the Household. This provides us with the socio-economic or social class
grouping to which the informant and the H.O.H. belong. Do not
use the phrase socio-economic group or social class to the
informant since it could lead to some misunderstanding on the
part of the informant.

We need to know it as one indication of the person's economic
and social standing. Naturally an occupation must be related to
education, income and other environmental factors of the person
concerned, and this is why you will be asking other classificatory
details besides occupation.

Explain why you want to know the informant's or the H.O.H.'s
occupation in general terms expressing the need for background
data, on lines suggested to you on pages 48, 110 & 139.

Our surveys are on matters of social and economic importance
and this being the case research workers in various fields often
wish to compare our findings with national statistics or the work
of other researchers in a similar field. Clearly if these comparisons are to be meaningful our data must be collected, analysed and presented in a similar way to these other statistics.

OCCUPATION

In order to classify occupations we use the Register General's
Classification of Occupations as used on the national Census of
the Population.

In this classification there are some two hundred main unit
groups of types of occupation, and further breakdown indicating
the socio-economic groups to which each occupation has been
assigned, and in most cases the degree of skill and/or qualifications required to do them. It also shows for each job whether
the work involved is mainly of a manual type or not.

In order to allow for such factors the classification consists
in all of some thirty thousand specific job descriptions which
are obviously far too many for you to learn off by heart. For
example there are some three hundred different codes from
which to choose if a person tells you he is "a cleaner" ranging
from whether he cleans airgates on drainage, or copper in a
brewery, or trays in a bakery, to pick but three of the three
hundred.

There are further distinctions to be made according to whether
persons are self-employed, or above works' foremen level of
management, or foremen, or labourers, or labourers with a
degree of skill.

Reference example 25 Layout for occupation and industry.

Occupation

(i)   In space for Occupation should be recorded the informant's name for his job and a clear description of the kind of work he does; the nature of the operation performed unless it is self-evident from the job title, e.g. dentist, bricklayer or carpenter.

It is not possible to devise any one question that will fit all cases, and the interviewer should adapt her approach to suit the situation.

EXAMPLE 25 OF OCCUPATION/INDUSTRY

(i) Occupation of H.O.H. (DESCRIBE FULLY)	OFF. USE
	i
(ii) Industry of H.O.H. (DESCRIBE FULLY)	
	ii
COMPLETE (a) and (b) BELOW ALSO (a) Self-employed or employee? Self-employed .... 1 Employee 2	
(b) IF MANAGER/SUPERINTENDENT OR SELF-EMPLOYED D.N.A. Not manager (etc.)............ A Number of employees in the establishment No: _____	

If the informant's description of his/her occupation is too technical or vague

"What kind of work is that?"

or

"What do you actually do in that job?"

are the most useful probes; but such questions are clearly absurd when the occupation is self-explanatory, e.g. dentist, ticket collector, or where the technical term for the job is well known, e.g. lino-type operator. On the other hand the interviewer should realise that certain terms that may present no difficulty to her because she is familiar with local industries may be incomprehensible to the staff at H.Q. and should therefore be explained. There are also certain occupations which, though they may appear to be self-explanatory, are not precise enough to permit of accurate classification. Some examples of these are given on page 128.

Industry (Trade or Profession)

(ii)   The heading **Industry** is a shortened heading meant to cover "trade" or "profession" as well as Industry. In the space (ii) should be recorded a clear description of the function of the informant's employer. You can tell the informant, as is the case, that we do not use the names of employers and that you will not even record it. What we want, and what you must ask the informant is *"what kind of a firm (is it) (do you work for)"* (firm here means the place where the informant works, which may be only a part of the firm).

If a person works for a very large and well known company it is still relevant to ask this question on what the firm does. Never merely record a firm's name or initials because you think coders will know what the firm does. You can say to your informant that naturally you have heard of the firm but may you check by asking them to tell you *"what is done at the (part) (branch) of the firm in which you work."*

When we say "What the firm does" we mean we want to know whether they manufacture or process at the establishment (and if so what). If the plant is not engaged in either manufacturing or processing we want to know its function, e.g. whether it is engaged in insurance, banking, wholesale or distributive trades, transport, civil engineering or some other activity.

NEITHER ON OCCUPATION NOR INDUSTRY, TRADE OR PROFESSION SHOULD YOU EVER PROMPT, i.e. never suggest categories of work, since an informant might merely agree with you because he did not know what the firm did.

Item (a)

Whether the person is self-employed, i.e. working on own account or as an employee, is straight forward since most persons know which kind of National Insurance contribution they have to pay (i.e. either all or part of the stamp). Note all directors of firms are employees, i.e. where a person turns his private business into a company he becomes an employee within it and should be coded as such. Note the codes at (a) tell us whether or not a person is self-employed. If he is self-employed we still need at item (i) (occupation) a clear job description, since a self-employed person can be anything from a working craftsman to a professional man or an administrator of office and works' staff.

Item (b)

This is an item we want asked for in this particular form, again, in order to code occupation as defined by the Registrar General. For any person who has indicated that he is in a managerial position at (i) (occupation), providing that he is self-employed and/or a manager or superintendent, i.e. above foreman level, ask (b), i.e. *"the number of people employed, in all capacities, in the establishment where you work".*

Job Details

It is essential to get a good description of the H.O.H.'s occupation as well as the informant's. A wife may be vague on the name for her husband's (H.O.H.'s) job, or quote an ambiguous title, yet she can usually give you a graphic description of what is involved in his job if you ask for it.

(1) An informant may say he is a Civil Servant. The first question to ask in this case is *"What is your grade?"* No further details are necessary for "occupation", unless the informant cannot tell you the grade, in which case *"What do you actually do?"* should be asked.

(2) It is not enough for somebody to answer "Engineer" as this can cover anything from a fully qualified professional employee with either a degree or an equivalent qualification to a semi-skilled machine operator. When an informant answers in vague terms like this, we in H.Q. would want to know what his full title was, and whether he was qualified professionally, e.g. "Professionally qualified – civil engineer (or electrical engineer etc.)". This means that the term "Engineer" **should never appear on its own unless** an informant cannot answer about another person's occupation any more exactly than this.

(3) Other vague job descriptions are "Machinist", "Technician", "Miner", "Collector" and "Laboratory Assistant". See notes below.

(a) MACHINIST

There are at least 1,000 different types of machinist and the socio-economic grouping and/or social class depends on the **type** of machinist. There are "Machine Grinders", "Machine Cutters", "Machine Casters", "Machine Drillers", etc. and obviously we want to know which **type** of machinist the informant is.

(b) TECHNICIAN

The term technician also has a wide range of usage and can be applied over almost the whole range of the social class and socio-economic groupings. Here we want to know whether the informant is e.g. a "Surgical Technician" or a "Radar Technician", a "Cine Technician" or any of the other approximately forty different types of technical worker ranging from the semi-professional type of worker down to a semi-skilled non-manual type of worker. This term is frequently used by informants to cover skilled types of worker such as an electrical fitter or a generating station attendant.

(c) MINERS

There are several types of miner. Some work at the coal face, underground and some are surface workers and the term miner can include "Coal Cutters", "Trimmers" (coal or coal **mine**) "Haulage Hand" etc. We always want to know his **full** job description and whether or not he works at the coal face.

(d) COLLECTORS

This term covers nearly 80 different types of worker. For example there are "Debt", "Rent", "Meter", "Rate" and "Salvage Collectors", or "Collectors of Custom and Excise", etc. etc. to name just a few.

(e) LABORATORY ASSISTANTS

Here again this occupation is used to describe someone who merely washes the utensils and instruments and cleans the laboratory generally. Whenever this occupation is given, describe fully the duties of the informant and any technical qualifications the informant may possess for this work.

As you can see these general headings like "Machinist" or "Miner" etc. **are not sufficient in themselves** and the fullest description should be given when such occupations are mentioned by the informant. You should consider whether what you have elicited gives you and coders a clear idea of how the informant spends a typical day, not minute by minute, but in terms of the skills he is using both mental and physical. Never suggest the type of job to the informant, always ask them to describe it in their own words.

Occupation/Industry details required in exceptional cases

Two or more jobs:

If the informant and/or H.O.H. has two or more jobs, details of the most remunerative should be recorded. (This differs from rule on no: of hours worked where in order to arrive at total no: of hours worked both jobs are taken into consideration.)

Unemployed persons

If a person is unemployed at the time of interview, i.e. if he is actively seeking work, record under occupation the number of months he has been unemployed followed by full details of his last occupation and industry.

Retired persons

Anyone beyond the normal retirement age who is no longer in paid employment will have been coded as Not Working and in the space reserved for details of paid occupation give the status of the person you have interviewed, i.e. "retired", together with a general description of his last main paid job. The "main" job is the one which the informant would consider his "career" job or in some cases whole working life-time job. Beside job details indicate person is retired (to explain the not working code which you will have ringed).

Other persons

Other persons coded Not Working (i.e. no paid work or only up to 10 hrs.) but not of retirement age should have their "status" recorded across occupation space.

- e.g. "housewife" or "housewife with only 5 hrs. private dress-making per week"

- or "Unoccupied – private means – never worked"

Item 8.

(a) SUMMARY DEFINITION OF INCOME

INCLUDE	
(employees)	(self-employed)
WAGES or SALARY including, overtime bonuses, tips	BUSINESS profit and salary
+ PENSIONS, old age, war, supplementary family allowances	
+ Sickness and unemployment benefits.	
+ Private means, stocks, shares, rents.	
+ regular contributions from persons living outside this household.	

EXCLUDE
Compulsory deductions for income tax, national insurance and graduated pension.
money transactions between members of **this** household (husband to wife, son to mother etc.)
drawings from savings (i. e. capital)

(b) SUMMARY ON PERIOD OF INCOME

If money from given sources comes	stress amount required is
(i) WEEKLY as WAGE	LAST WEEKS
(ii) MONTHLY, 3, or 6 MONTHLY	all sources into account and AVERAGE per week
(iii) ANNUALLY as SELF-EMPLOYED	total annual profit considered to give AVERAGE per week

Item 8. INCOME

On most surveys we need to know the informant's income, within a given range. You are not required to ask the informant for the actual sum, but before asking him to indicate into which range his income falls you must tell him

(a) the types of income you want him to include and exclude from the sum.

(b) the period of time over which he is to consider his income.

A list is given below of the items which should be included and excluded from a person's income. The list is for your guidance. It must be learnt so that during each interview you can give all informants an explanation of what we mean by the term income.

(a) TYPE OF INCOME

INCLUDE IN INCOME

(a) All earnings.

(b) Overtime payments, bonuses and tips.

(c) Profits and salary from business.

(d) All kinds of pensions.

(e) Ministry of Social Security, sickness and unemployment benefits.

(f) Family allowances (credit it to the mother of the child(ren)).

(g) Private means received from investments and rent from properties.

(h) Payments from *lodgers and relatives, etc. who are **not** members of the household, and Forces allowances.

(*NB. the term Lodgers we use to signify persons who cater for themselves.)

EXCLUDE FROM INCOME

(a) Money transactions from members of the household one to another (e.g. housekeeping money from husband to the housewife; money received in return for board and lodging, whether from members of the family or three or less boarders).

(N.B. Boarders as defined in the definition of household.)

(b) Amounts drawn from saving or capital.

(c) Income tax and social security deductions from earnings.

(d) Compulsory superannuation and graduated pension contributions from earnings.

(Note: Voluntary deductions from pay, for savings or clubs, do not count as exclusions.)

On many surveys the interviewer is provided with a card on which income groups are set out. In such a case the card is shown to the informant, whilst the interviewer explains what she would like included and excluded from income.

(On some surveys we need full details of the informant's income from each particular source. These cases will be explained to the interviewers as they occur at specific survey briefings.)

The income card is devised to make the question go smoothly. If other people are present during the interview your informant might not want them to know his income, though he would not mind telling you. You hand him the card and explain its use, that we have put sums of money into different groups on the card and would like to know his income from all sources. Tell him that he does not need to give us the actual amount but only to mention the code number of the category into which his income falls.

EXAMPLE 26 OF LAYOUT FOR INCOME:			
NETT INCOME last week (Show Card)			
(a) Income of INFORMANT – (Sjt.) (b) " " H.O.H. (Last Week)	(Per Year)	(a) Sjt.	(b) H.O.H.
NIL	NIL	0	0
up to £7.10.	(Up to £390)	1	1
over £7.10. to £10	(Over £390 to £520)	2	2
over £10 to £12.10.	(Over £520 to £650)	3	3
over £12.10 to £15	(Over £650 to £780)	4	4
over £15 to £20	(Over £780 to £1040)	5	5
over £20 to £25	(Over £1040 to £1300)	6	6
over £25 to £30	(Over £1300 to £1560)	7	7
over £30	(Over £1560 –	8	8
D.K.		9	9
Refusal/Not asked		X	X
If code 9 or X give reason;			

If the informant (subject) is the same person as the H.O.H. loopcode the answer code.

(Example) Over £7.10 to £10   (2   2)

PERIOD OF TIME OVER WHICH TO CONSIDER INCOME

Weekly incomed persons

If an income card is being used and the income shown on the card is in weekly amounts it should be made clear to all weekly incomed informants that what is required is **income** for the **last week, from all sources.** We do not want them to average out their earnings since we will produce averages of incomes from the data provided.

An example of what you might say to obtain this information from a **weekly incomed** person is: *"What was your income last week from all sources, including any wages, overtime, bonuses and any private income which you might receive, but excluding Income Tax and other compulsory deductions from pay?"* To this simplest form of basic question it is necessary to add other items as you think that they might apply. For instance, to a housewife you may need to explain that you do not want her to include the housekeeping money she receives from her husband. An elderly informant you would ask to include any pensions he receives, but to exclude withdrawals from savings. In this way you are relating further prompting of sources to your particular informant. By drawing his attention to possible sources in this way you will gain a more accurate account of total income.

Monthly incomed persons

If the informant receives income at some interval other than a weekly interval ask him to decide into which of these groups his average weekly income is most likely to fall, taking into consideration all his sources of income. In his case to press for details of money received last week would be misleading, since whatever he received would not represent strictly his income for that week.

For a **salaried person** you could say:

"Would you look at this card on which we've shown amounts of money per week. Can you tell me into which group per week you think your net income is likely to come, taking into account your salary (although this is not a weekly amount) and any overtime or bonuses you may receive, together with any private means or pensions (if you have any), but after Income Tax and other compulsory deductions."

Self-employed persons

To a **self-employed person** you could say:

*"On this card we show various amounts of money. Normally
we are asking weekly-incomed people to say what their income
was for last week but in the case of someone like yourself who
is self-employed we would like you to look at the card and say
into which group your income falls if averaged out per week. By
income I mean the total income you received from the business,
i.e. any money you draw out of the business weekly, plus any
money you have as profits at the end of the year. Also include
as income, money from other sources such as: private means;
stocks; any rents, and pensions, but after any deductions for
Income tax or Social Security payments, and not including money
from other people living here with you".*

In the case of a **self-employed** person it is particularly important to make clear that you want income from all sources to be
taken into consideration. He will have to think back, probably,
to the most recent accounting period for which he has received
figures of profits etc., and to look at the income card and consider, in the light of these figures, which is the most appropriate
weekly group. To ask for a weekly income of such p ople,
without explanation, is difficult and misleading, since a small
businessman might well, in error, give the amount of money he
draws weekly from his business as his weekly income, whereas
his total income may well be made up of weekly drawings plus an
additional annual profit.

Income of H.O.H.

In cases where we require income data for the Head of Household
and your informant is not the H.O.H., if the Head of Household
is present at the time of interview you should obtain the information direct from him rather than from the person being interviewed.
Remember to explain first the need for asking H.O.H.'s income.
If the person being interviewed is not the Head of Household,
and if the Head of Household is not present at the interview,
there is a ruling on the circumstances in which one asks the
informant to discuss the Head of Household's income.

The ruling is to ask for income about another person only if
the person being interviewed is in one of the following relationships to him: HUSBAND, WIFE, FATHER, MOTHER, SON,
DAUGHTER, BROTHER, SISTER (by blood, in-law or adoption).
This is a general ruling. In any household where relationships
are estranged do not jeopardise the goodwill established in the
interview by asking for such data about the Head of Household of
another person. In any such case show the question was not
asked and record the reason for omission. In cases where the
informant is only distantly related to the Head of Household and
you know by the above rule that you cannot ask for the H.O.H.'s
income code "Not Asked" (x in our example on page 131) and
write in the reason in the space provided, i.e. *"not in right
relationship".*

Item 9. TYPE OF DWELLING

On many, but not all surveys we need to know something about the dwelling in which your informant lives. You may be asked to use the following categories:

EXAMPLE 27 TYPE OF DWELLING	
Whole house – detached	1
– semi-detached (inc. prefab)	2
– terrace	3
Flat/Maisonette-self-contained	4
Rooms	5
Caravan	6
Other type of dwelling (specify)	7

A house which is the end house of a terrace is to be coded as a terraced house (code 3 in the example).

The distinction between flat, self-contained (code 4) and rooms (code 5) is that the former has all its rooms contained behind one door, whereas a dwelling classed as rooms does not.

Item 10. NUMBER OF ROOMS

You will be told for each specific survey whether or not bathrooms are to be in or excluded from the count of the total number of rooms available to the household. Frequently you will be told by informants they have a kitchen, which they may refer to as a scullery or a living room rather than a kitchen. It is important to avoid counting any room twice or to omitting it altogether. Whenever you are in doubt write out full details of the rooms by name.

Frequently the research officer will advise you per survey on what to include as a "room"; most often it will be decided on size, though sometimes by function.

Age at which finished full-time education

It is sometimes important to know the age at which the informant left his full time school (in the majority of cases this will be between the ages of 13 years – 18 years although there can be exceptions). An example of schedule layout is shown below.

Note you cannot assume the age when his formal schooling ended from knowing the type of school the informant attended.

On a question such as this where memory is involved you must follow the usual practice and ask for an exact age. If he says he cannot remember then probe for an estimate. If he says, for example, he was about 17 years but cannot remember if under or over, write in the answer to the left of the codes and put "e" for "estimate" beside the appropriate code number.

EXAMPLE 28		
Age at which Sjt. completed full-time schooling		
		CODE
GAPS OF ANY LENGTH DUE TO ILLNESS AND OF 3 MONTHS OR LESS FOR ANY OTHER REASON, SHOULD BE IGNORED.	14 and under	....1 ..
	15 but under 16	....2 ..
	16 but under 17	....3 ..
	17 but under 18	....4 ..
	18 and over	....5 ..

Item 11. TYPE OF EDUCATION

On many opinion surveys it is relevant to know the type of school last attended either by the informant or by his parents. The example given overleaf is perhaps the most usual way of grouping schools.

EXAMPLE 29

Type of school attended last by sjt. for full-time formal education.

	Sjt.
Secondary modern/elementary/non-grammar denominational schools	1
Post 1947 Comprehensive schools	2
Pre-1947 Central/Intermediate/higher grade......	3
Technical School/Tech: college (up to and including age of 18)	4
State Grammar/or Grammar type/County High/ Free 1947 Senior Secondary School...............	5
Private Direct Grant/Grammar/public school	6
Private commercial schools/colleges (up to and including age of 18)	7
All Foreign schools including Eire (up to and including age of 18)	8
Other answer (specify, mentioning whether state or private)	X

Further Education

Sometimes research officers wish to know about further education. The amount of detail required for this may vary from survey to survey, but the definition of further education is generally defined as education pursued at establishments other than the schools mentioned above.

EXAMPLE 30

Further Education of Subject i. e. since leaving school.

Count: (i) only if course pursued for at least one session (i. e. one academic year, or 3 terms) or longer.

       (ii) Professional, academic, commercial, trade, vocational.

(Exclude: purely leisure courses.)

	Sjt.
Full-time course in university, college, other educational institution	1
Full apprenticeship completed (S.R.N. completed)	2
Part-time/correspondence course pursued ...	3
No further education...........................	4

Item 12. EDUCATIONAL QUALIFICATIONS

The establishment attended does not necessarily indicate educational attainment and so you may be asked to check separately for qualifications obtained by the informant.

Whilst you are meant to find out the exact qualification, in order to decide into which category it belongs, note you are not meant to use as a prompt the qualifications listed below. Anything mentioned which is similar though not identical to a qualification listed below should be recorded fully under 'other specify' 8.

EXAMPLE 31

Qualifications obtained by subject

GIVE HIGHEST QUALIFICATION ONLY, EXCLUDE APPRENTICESHIP	CODE
No qualification obtained	1 ...
University degree, higher degree (including full medical training)	2 ...
Higher National Certificate or Diploma	3 ...
Teachers Certificate, Membership of a professional institute, Full or intermediate professional qualifications, S.R.N., G.C.E., 'A' level, Higher School Certificate, Intermediate (Arts/Science)	4 ...
Ordinary National Certificate or Diploma	5 ...
G.C.E., 'O' level, Matriculation, General School Certificate, City and Guilds, R.S.A., Forces Educational Certificates, Commercial or Trade certificates/diplomas	6 ...
D.K.	7 ...
Other SPECIFY below	8 ...

....

EXCEPTIONS TO STANDARD RULING

As mentioned at the beginning of this chapter the above definitions of classification items stand UNLESS SPECIFIC INSTRUCTIONS TO THE CONTRARY are given, in the special instructions for a particular survey.

For specialist enquiries such as the Family Expenditure Survey it is necessary to employ different definitions even for fundamental concepts such as Household, Working and Income, and these are explained fully in the instructions for such specialist surveys.

IT IS ESSENTIAL TO RE-STUDY STANDARD DEFINITIONS AFTER WORKING ON ANY STUDY CONTAINING NON-STANDARD DEFINITIONS.

The general ruling on the need to explain to your informant the purpose of classification applies on **all** surveys.

GENERAL POINTS

It is bad to use any phrase or tone of voice that suggests you are apologetic about asking for data in an interview, as this suggests you doubt the informant's willingness to answer. (Too many *"may I ask you's"* may bring a retort that you may not.) However, there is a use for polite phrases from time to time, not voiced diffidently, but in order to show that you are not taking it wholly for granted that this is a straight question and answer routine. Remember throughout the need to keep the informant at ease whilst he is answering classificatory questions. If he is clear about the necessity for us to have a picture of the person who has expressed views on the subject matter of the survey, then you will find him willing and helpful in giving facts about himself.

Just as on any other question on a schedule if an informant says he prefers not to answer a classification question there can be no compulsion for him to do so. Do explain if he asks whether he must give a reply, that he is not forced to, but go on to explain why the question is relevant. Most often this will lead to the informant giving you the answer. Remember that an interview on which your informant refused to complete the classification section wholly would be useless to us since we would not be able to compare his responses on the subject matter of the survey with anyone else's responses since we would not know whether we were comparing like with like person or not.

SUMMARY OF POINTS FROM CLASSIFICATION SECTION

(i) CLASSIFICATION IS BACKGROUND DATA ON THE
     INFORMANT; factors which it is held generally influence
     one's outlook and way of life. All surveys aim to
     discover which types of people behave or think in which
     ways and the researcher wants to be able to see how
     the different sections of the community are affected
     by government policies.

     EXPLAIN purpose of classification questions in simple
     words to the informant. Tell him of our need to relate
     given views or facts on the subject matter of the survey
     to the kinds of people who have been interviewed. Names
     do not help us on this, we do not use names in our
     report. It is sensible for us to take into account the
     ages, sizes of family and like factors which describe
     to us the person who has been interviewed.

(ii) AVOID use of JARGON, i.e. if our terms for items are
      used without explanation they will be misconstrued,
      since we have attached uncommon, specific definitions
      to them.

(iii) LEARN definitions and then APPLY them clearly in
      each interview:

      Household — group of people living regularly under
                   same roof, sharing same catering
                   arrangements, i.e. meal a day together
                   provided from same source.

      Housewife — resident, person mainly responsible
                   for domestic duties.

      H.O.H.   — resident, in whose name house is owned
                   or rented (or one who is allowed to live
                   there rent free).

      Occupation — description of what informant actually
                   does in job.

      Industry   — description of firm's function + nos:
                   employed when above job is supervisory.

      Income   — all sources if weekly   — last
                     "   "   if other periods — average
                     "   "   if own business — drawing +
                                                    profit
                                                    averaged
                                                    out.

Chapter 12

SUMMARY ON METHOD

Throughout interviews you need to keep in mind that there are certain basic sources of error that can occur in verbal communication to upset the collection of accurate data.

(a) All of us when talking to others spend some energy or devote some of our attention to finding out the motives of the other person, and we try to see how these fit in with our own needs (which can include a desire on our part to create an impression on the other person). There is an evaluation and classification of what is being said on both sides, and so unconsciously we often hear only what we wish to hear.

(b) As adults we are experienced in communicating with others, and so we guess in advance what is being said to us and fail to hear what is actually said; possibly we guess incorrectly.

(c) There may be a psychological barrier between the informant and the information we want. He may have little knowledge on the subject, he may have forgotten what we want to know about. If the question put to an informant touches on a subject painful to him to discuss, it may be that he will either not answer at all, saying or thinking he does not remember, or be evasive, or even if pressed, wrongly, give false information. There is no uniform guide to memory faults.

(d) Language. One may meet foreign speaking people, people who speak heavy dialect or groups of the public who have some difficulty in self-expression, when you are wanting them to put their experience or reasons for actions into words.

Some of the sources of error listed above apply to you as well as to the informant, item (b) in particular.

Error in communication can be cut by careful planning of the interviews, by using as we do, tested questions which have proved most meaningful to the majority of people.

This schedule of questions is a tool to help you collect accurate data. As with all tools it is important to know how to use the schedule. Practise until you can use it so well that you do not have to consider its use, but can concentrate on the object on which you work. Your object is your informant.

In order to have time to concentrate on your informant's reaction to questions, you must learn to scan a schedule before field work begins: consider the scope of each question, study where particular series of questions occur and which topic leads on from another. If you do this, and memorise in which circumstances questions do and do not apply, you will know enough about the form of the interview to conduct it smoothly in the field. Some interviewers find reading a schedule out loud is one way of learning its form.

Realise there is a plan to the sequence of topics introduced into an interview. Questions that tax the informant tend to be left until a point in the interview by which, we assume, a good relationship will have been built up between yourself and the informant.

Some topics may be re-introduced in a different way at a later stage in an interview to help us gauge the informant's opinion more accurately. Methodical handling of the questions, progressing by number is essential, but it must never seem wooden to your informant. Know your schedule until the questions come over as spontaneous speech.

Question order and circumstances in which it may/may not be changed

Often an informant may mention an area you want to question him about later in the interview. If he does this indicate that what he is telling you is something in which you are interested and about which you would like to know more later on. This will often enable you to get on with current questioning. When you then reach the appropriate questions you can preface them with the comment

"I think you mentioned something about this earlier"

and then go on to the actual questions. So long as acknowledgement of past comments is made in this way informants will not feel you are disregarding anything they say.

When you do come to the actual question on no account put down what the informant formerly said; to do so would be to **forward code** replies, and the cases where precise questions are answered before asked are few and far between. When your **actual** question is put the informant may wish to make a different point.

If earlier in the interview you failed to stop the informant from talking about the later issue, if he expressed himself at length on it because it was something about which he felt strongly, you should note in the margin where this happened (quoting what he said). Then, at the appropriate place in the interview, try the gambit,

"You did tell me something about this. I was going to ask (the question)." Alternatively one could try, *"What was it you did say about (the question)...?"*

If the question produces only a sparse reply which you cannot get him to clarify, because he remembers having detailed it to you already, one needs to say something on the lines

"You did mention something about this before of course, now what was it you said?",

as though you cannot remember it all. If he will not, or cannot be expected to repeat all he said, you must make a note in the margin to this effect and give the earlier question number so that coders can refer back to his response.

142

If the data to carry forward is factual and if, for example, the informant has told you during the interview, he is married or has children, you should still use the check form of question

"I believe you told me, but may I check ... (the question)".

This form of checking is necessary because the informant may be answering on different premises. Someone may refer to his children and include those no longer at home whereas we may be wanting to know only the number living at this address.

Circumstances in which responses to earlier questions may/ may not be changed

You do not go back and change or query the answer already given to an OPINION question should the informant contradict himself on a later question — not even if asked to do so by the informant. At some stage of the interview he may want to change his view as a result of the line of questioning you have pursued since the time of asking him the earlier question. Note where, and how, he asks for a reversal of response, if he does, but leave the original reply intact.

On the other hand you must check for consistency in FACTUAL questions. You need a retentive mind throughout the interview. As you come to ask subsequent questions, remember what has gone before, both in answer to your factual questioning and from incidental conversation with the informant. If you feel there has been contradiction in his factual responses, it is your job to reconcile the answers.

Do this by suggesting that you (the interviewer) may not have made a point clear and ask if you can go back over it. The informant may answer in a different way this time because he had genuinely misunderstood the question the first time. Or if, at the earlier stage of the interview, he had felt disinclined to give you precise data (without indicating this was the case) your reference back to the question, in terms of there being an error on **your** part, will give him the opportunity to amend an answer without loss of face.

SEQUENCE OF AN

INTERVIEW

FIELD		
BUILD UP AND CONTINUANCE OF CONTACT WITH INFORMANT	(xii) use direct questions, based on thorough knowledge of survey definitions. Follow instructions on probing and prompting techniques.	
	(xiii) record replies accurately and swiftly.	
	(xiv) reassure, and be informative to informant whilst maintaining a pleasant yet business like approach throughout.	
	(xv) control the interview: putting questions at a speed to suit the informant.	
END OF CONTACT	(xvi) Before leaving informant look through schedule for completeness and/or need for further questions.	
	(xvii) give thanks for co-operation and add further words on value/purpose of the material.	

(CHECKING)

After interview inspect schedule

own HOME	Within hour or so	1 day later
	(xviii) for complete coding and legibility.	(xxi) re-check schedule, without memory of informant's tone. If response unclear add further notes for coders.
	(xix) identifying number and own name on schedule.	(xxii) Despatch schedule to H.Q. on this the day after interview.
	(xx) add: explanation of unusual circumstances.	

SEQUENCE OF AN INTERVIEW

PLACE	(STAGE)	TASKS	
		(a) **Study of:**	(b) **Preparation of:**
own	(PREPARATORY) H O M E	(i) **sample instructions.**	(vi) schedules, prompt cards in order of use, auth: card, pencils, and leaflets.
		(ii) **types of questions** on schedule and consideration of basic way of handling each.	(vii) planning economic route for visiting quota of addresses. Preparing appointments sheet.
		(iii) any **non-standard instructions** for specific questions.	(viii) address of police station, to visit before starting quota.
		(iv) **layout of schedules** memorising how sections and questions interleave.	
		(v) purpose of survey, to determine introductions on it.	
	(INTERVIEW) THE APPROACH	(ix) Identify the sampled person.	
		(x) **Give purpose of survey:** name of client; name of our Department; methods of selection; mention confidentiality and time factor. (Part of this on doorstep and part inside house).	
		(xi) Show authorisation card.	

Chapter 13

ALLOCATION OF FIELD WORK

Our overall field dates and estimated cost of field work are based on our experience of the length of the interview from the pilot study for the survey and on our prior knowledge of costs for past similar type surveys.

From the above we can assess how many interviews per day we can expect to achieve.

In allocating field work we have to take into account

(a) the number of interviewers available to work in the current month, in the areas which have been selected for our sample

and

(b) the number of days per week that each of you is prepared to work. We must know the precise number of days in order to decide whether one, two or three interviewers are needed to cover the size quota per area. The above information we get from your Availability forms.

Every quarter you are asked to fill in two Availability Forms, stating when you are free to work during the coming six months and telling us of any periods within the dates when you will not be free to undertake any work.

Opposite is an example of the form you are asked to complete. In item 1, where you are asked to quote the number of days available it is to be clearly understood that a day also includes an evening.

Since each form covers a three-month period, your availability may change after you have completed and returned the form to us. We take care of this on the long term basis by sending out forms each quarter, so that you are revising your six month's availability every third month. However you availability may become greater or less for one of the first three months in question. **We want you to notify us of all changes in your availability the minute they occur.** The more the allocating officer knows of you availability or domestic commitments the easier it will be for her to allocate work economically.

EXAMPLE OF AVAILABILITY FORM

PLEASE REPLY BY RETURN

GOVERNMENT SOCIAL SURVEY

QUARTERLY RETURN OF INTERVIEWER AVAILABILITY

Period covered (mth:)____19___ to   (mth:)____19___

1 On an average how many days a week can you work during the next three months?

2 Are there any dates or periods during the next three months when you will be unable to work? If so please give details.

3 If required would you normally be able to stay away from home during the next three months? If so, for how long at a time and how much notice would you need to make arrangements?

4 Are there any areas for which you have a special preference? (Give areas)

Interviewer Name .... Auth: no:

Home address ....

....

We aim to distribute work fairly amongst available field staff. This is dependent on our having up-to-date records from you on the amount of time you can give us. Retrospectively we convert your availability into a work history, setting your stated availability against what it was shown to be when you were set a task. It is no use stating you can give us the minimum requirement of three days and evenings each week if, in fact, for one or two of the weeks out of the month you could never be free three whole days, running into the evening. Any occasional restrictions on availability, a temporary need to be home for meals or at other times of the day, **must** be given, so that we can accurately code you as not available for any month whilst you are so restricted.

Our starting date for a survey is set according to when we know the previous survey is due to be out of the field. Once we know the number of areas that have to be covered on a survey and how many interviewers are available, we estimate the number of weeks the survey will need to be in the field. Sometimes the number of interviewers per area which we use depends on whether the survey can stay in the field more than a minimum number of weeks. If it is an opinion study usually we need to have it out of the field as soon as possible, since changes in current events or news features may affect people's responses on the subject of our survey. Once we have decided on the field dates we must adhere to them because the Coding and Computing Branches' work on the survey follows on from our field work. These other specialist sections must know when work will begin to come in from the field and by which date it will all be in. They have to arrange to have the appropriate number of people ready to work on the survey.

The programme of work in different specialist sections does not dovetail easily, since any one survey demands a different amount of attention at different stages. For example, a short interview may require lengthy coding, whereas a long interview which is heavily precoded may take correspondingly less of coders' time. Any delay in the field programme can create a lot of trouble for other sections. One week longer in the field may result in a research officer getting his tables from Computing Branch some one or two months later than the estimated date, due to the way we have delayed or disorganised Coding or Computing staff by over-running our field completion date.

OFFER OF WORK

You are sent several details about a forthcoming survey: the area in which it will occur, field dates, the name of the survey and the date on which you should attend H. Q. for briefing. The nature of the survey will be apparent from the survey's name. Often you are told nothing more than the name at this stage. The area in which you are asked to work may or may not be one which you have given us as an area for which you have a preference. Sometimes you may be offered a quota in an area which is an hour's travelling distance from your home. If it is this far, or farther, when accepting the quota do mention the distance to us. On the map the area may appear to be nearer than this and it may be local transport conditions which will extend travelling time and make the quota a difficult one for you.

We try to allocate work to the interviewers living nearest to the areas which occur on our sample. This is not always possible. Sampling Branch select areas on a random basis so as to be representative of the population. This is done without thought of where interviewers live. This, the chance of where the sample falls, together with other factors such as inter- viewers' suitability for certain types of surveys, and the fact that we have several surveys in the field at the same time, sometimes result in our offering you a quota of work which is one hour's travelling distance from your home.

Since in some cases it is costly to get you to the sampled area we rely on you, once there, to put in a good day's work, in order to reduce the number of days on which you need to travel to and from the area.

When we offer you work you must reply immediately saying whether or not you accept it. If you do not write the allocating officer may decide silence means non-acceptance and offer the work to someone else. She will have to do this if you do not write and acknowledge work because she must provide an interviewer for each area, she must check on the total number of interviewers there are to brief and she must know which of you will be working on the survey in order that we can decide which of you are due for field supervision and need to be fitted into one or other training officer's programme for the forth- coming month. To avoid missing work because you are away from home always send us temporary addresses when you are on holiday etc. You can then receive invitations for work to be done on your return home.

Our allocation of work has to occur a month before the survey is due to be fielded. We do like you to accept the briefing date whenever possible, but if you cannot accept it when you accept the quota of work tell us on which other dates you would be free. **You must attend a briefing on a survey before you can do any field work on that survey.**

MATERIALS FOR SURVEY

Any material you need for a survey will be sent to your home before field work starts. It is your responsibility to check that the documents you receive are correct and that you have enough schedules to cover the number of addresses on which you must call. If there is a discrepancy you should notify the office at once.

STUDY TIME

You are allowed several hours study time for each survey. Before coming to the briefing you are expected to use some of these hours for reading the instructions and looking through the schedule. This is so that the research officer and group of interviewers can concentrate on the more complex parts of the interview at the briefing, without spending time going through every detail of the schedule or instructions. The research officer will expect you to query with him any item you did not understand from your reading of the instructions at home. **It cannot be over-emphasised how important it is for you to put in at least as many hours study as we have offered you, before you go out on that survey.** Research officers are advised by field section of the amount of study time to give per survey and this we decide from our own perusal of the schedules. The number of hours is no more than the number we consider it essential to spend on the documents.

What takes place at the briefing has been described in Chapter 3.

DUMMIES

In order to familiarise yourself further with the schedule you will often be asked to complete one or two "dummy" or trial interviews before attempting to interview anyone on your real quota. This is to ensure that the interviews with any sampled person will include no inaccuracies due to unfamiliarity with the schedule; you will resolve these at your trial address(es).

Sometimes we supply special addresses for the purpose. Often we leave it that you decide on which doors to knock. On no account do you mention the words dummy or trial to the informant. The interview has to be conducted in the same way as at any sampled address. You send these interviews in to us at once. You may be asked to do no further work until you get dummies back with coder's comments. Whether you can work on your actual addresses before the dummies are returned to you depends on the complexity of the survey.

Chapter 14

INTERVIEWER PLANNING AND CONTACT WITH H.Q.

FIELD WORK

Once you have been briefed and are ready to start on your field quota:

1 Plan your work well in an attempt to get through the greatest number of interviews per day

Adequate use of a map for finding addresses and knowledge of local bus timetables result in one having no unnecessary, undirected walking about the district. You should look at the day's work and consider the ratio of time you have spent travelling to actually interviewing. Decide whether it is a fair day's work. We know that in order to interview accurately and get a true random sample you may have to spend a disproportionate amount of time on some addresses. **We trust you to work in the most efficient way that is compatible with the most accurate way.** Many maps are kept in the office and you should ask us to send one if you do not already have one of the area in which you have been asked to work. On completion of the quota send the map back to Field Service. Mark your streets etc. in pencil, not pen, so that before returning the map to H.Q. you can rub out which streets you had marked so that the map can be passed on to and used by another interviewer.

Method of transportation

Some of you will work by public transport and some by use of own car. You must plan your coming day's calls with the aid of a map no matter which form of transport you will be using. If you are a car user your work would be most uneconomic if you did not plan a route. Without planning work you would clock up many unnecessary miles during the day. If you are a mobile interviewer, or sent some distance from home to a rural area where you find that public transport services are negligible, then you must discover what other facilities there are in the area. Can you hire a local taxi or is there a self-drive hire car? When you have found out what exists telephone H.Q. and tell us of your findings. It is your responsibility to seek out different forms of transport and to show us which is the most economic. Quote rates etc. to us for mileage and/or waiting time and we will then tell you whether or not we can authorise the expenditure.

2 Prepare an Appointments Sheet

Copy into your notebook or diary the addresses on which you are about to call.   Check that you have copied the addresses correctly.   We cannot afford to have an error on house numbers etc.   You need to use a copy list of some kind in order to have figures on the total numbers of calls, contacts and non-contacts made each day.   You need data of this kind in order to:

(a) enter it on your expense sheet each day.   (Instructions explaining how and what you can claim by way of expenses and fees are provided by Administration Branch.)

(b) enable you to know when you formerly called on people; what took place at the call, what time of day it was.   It will show you, at a glance, what appointments you have lined up with them for remaining days and evenings in the coming weeks.

(c) assist anyone who might have to take over your quota, if by some misfortune you are unable to complete it.   It would be invaluable for them to know which addresses you had called on to date and what appointments there were to be kept by them.

3 Call at the local police station which covers the area in which you are about to work

We will give you a form to leave with the police.   It states the name of the survey and how long you will be in the area.   Any other interviewer joining you must make her own call on the police and similarly give the dates in which she will be in the area.   If you expect to be supervised on a quota add the name of training officer to your own form and say Miss X will be with you for only part of the period.   Show your authorisation card to the police.   Ensure that they enter details of your call in their "day book" whilst you are still there.

4 Cover all given addresses in the shortest possible time

You need to bear field dates in mind so as to avoid over-running them.   You need to keep survey costs down by looking up the addresses on a map (as stated at 1) so that you can call on them in the easiest geographical order.   An occasional survey will have an instruction to approach people in address list order, but this is exceptional and it would be made known to you at the briefing for the survey on which it was to be done.   You will have been given a finishing date for your quota.   For many surveys a four-week field period is allowed, this is to afford you the chance of interviewing everybody you set out to interview.   You should **aim to call on all the addresses within two, if not one week, from the beginning of the field period.**   If you do this it means from the date on which you first call on a person there is at least two weeks of field time left. You can then recall again and again if necessary. You have the chance of catching up with people who say initially *"I am too busy this week"*, or with people who happen to be ill, or on holiday during the week of your first call.

The last week of a quota is meant for mopping up the last few interviews with people you have been trying very hard to get for several weeks. Knowing the number of weeks at your disposal it follows that **you** must tell **us** if your work is not progressing well. Your quota will usually be of a size which we expect you can cover, in the number of days you have said you will be available. If for **any** reason you cannot work for several days, **you must notify the office.** Similarly if you are working long hours, but failing to find people at home, we must be told that this is happening. If many of you have to tell us of delays we will have to discuss the matter with the research officer and coding section to decide whether or not we can let any survey over-run set field dates. We can only take action if you have contacted us and told us of likely delays.

5 Send in work regularly and at most within two days of its field completion

Payment of any claim for expenses cannot be authorised until we have received and checked your field work for all the days to which the claim refers. We know the difficulties of working flat out and yet having time to check documents, and this is why we allow two rather than one day between completion of interview and its return to H.Q. You ought never to delay checking schedules more than one day after the interview. You cannot adequately remember interview details at more than one day's remove and you must check whilst you remember in order to add any necessary explanatory notes. Sending schedules back to us quickly serves yet another useful purpose in that they can be prechecked by Coding Section (i.e. looked through for errors and omissions). If any errors are found, the schedules can be sent back to you for recall at the address and before you have completed much more of your quota and repeated any mistakes.

Despatch notes are provided and should be included with each packet of schedules posted to H.Q. You will need to keep a note yourself of the date on which each schedule was despatched, in case we need to query it with you. Take extra care in adding serial numbers to schedules and despatch notes. We have the task of checking off your returns against our copy address list. On a despatch note, in addition to recording the numbers of interviews achieved, you must account for all non-contacts.

An actual example of a despatch note is not given here as despatch notes differ slightly for each survey. Space is allowed on them for you to write in the actual serial numbers of the addresses with which you have dealt since your last return.

A minimum of two despatch notes must be in the post from you to us each week whilst you hold a quota of work. If necessary, put on it an explanatory note as to why more work has not been done in the period.

Your despatch note will itemise:

(i)   The no: of interviews enclosed

(ii)   Any non-contacts (together with the type they are − see below)

(iii)   A check of the no: of addresses in quota set

(iv)   The no: referred to in this despatch (i & ii)

(v)   The no: still outstanding

NON-RESPONSE

A NON-CONTACT (ITEM ii) IS AN ADDRESS/NAMED PERSON ON THIS SURVEY FOR WHICH IT IS CLEAR YOU ARE WHOLLY UNABLE TO ACHIEVE AN INTERVIEW

It can be an address at which:

(a)   you have called morning, noon and night **on different** days, in **different** weeks throughout the whole four weeks of the field period. But you have never succeeded in finding anyone at home.

(b)   on a named **person** sample, when you visit the address you are told the named person is dead.

       (A non-contact is never an address where no-one is in today, but on which you intend to recall later in the period, that is simply a "call".)

(c)   you have seen the eligible person but he tells you he has no intention what-so-ever of taking part in any survey or else he makes an appointment to see you but is out on your recall. If you cannot interview someone you have seen this is a REFUSAL.

We must lose as few people as possible from our sample. Further, we must know who we are losing and for what reasons. We rely on **you** to give us an account of your attempts to get people and a full explanation of who and why you lost anyone.

This means that for (a), (b) or (c) cases you must give:

(i)   the number of calls made at the address (with times of day, and in which weeks calls occurred).

(ii)   who you did or did not see at the address.

(iii) whatever information you have on sex, possible age and type of household/person you were meant to see.

additionally, in the case of (a) non-contact:

(iv)   the known or judged reason why they were not at home during the period.

in the case of (c) a refusal:

(v)   the terms in which you introduced the survey to the informant, his stated reason for refusal and your assessment of real reason, if different.

6 Notify Field Branch if work is not proceeding to plan, in any respect

A widely scattered field force makes good liaison between interviewers and the office essential. Remember you are never farther away from H.Q. than the nearest telephone or letter box and if you have any field worries contact us immediately.

How else can you help us achieve this contact?

You can achieve contact by:

(a) replying promptly to letters and telegrams.

(b) contacting us immediately anything goes wrong at an address. If you leave an address feeling uneasy as to the manner an informant adopted with you, tell us about it. A query may arise from the person in question or from a member of his family and if we know your side of the story beforehand it is easier to answer the informant's query on your behalf.

If you:

(c) have any queries from local press reporters whilst you are in the field, show them your authorisation card. It bears our telephone number. Tell them they can get in touch with H.Q. if they want to know about our survey. You should not give them any details about the survey on which you are working. But again, telephone us and tell us of the encounter and that an enquiry may be on its way.

(d) let us know if your sample list, by chance, contains the name of any person known to you. Hand back his name and address to us for reallocation to another interviewer. Whilst you may feel no embarrassment at questioning an acquaintance he may well be unable to accept the fact that our sample was random and the survey confidential if you are known to him.

(e) have a query about work (a grouse or a problem) ring or write us about it rather than contact another interviewer in your area. We are in daily contact with research staff, we deal with queries from, and have trained hundreds of interviewers, so advice from us is "straight from the horse's mouth" and far better than Mrs. Y's, who has no more contact with H.Q. than you do.

(f) Any member of the public or an acquaintance of yours who wants to know more about our organisation than you feel qualified to mention should be put in touch with us. This does not imply that many people should be referred to H.Q. As a trained interviewer you are expected to know enough about the Government Social Survey's role to answer all lay questions yourself. **Do not discuss current surveys with your friends.** Mention instead surveys we have carried out which you know have been publicly reported and which are therefore available to them.

REMEMBER YOU DO NOT TELL ANYBODY ELSE THE NAME OF ANYONE YOU HAVE INTERVIEWED ON OUR BEHALF, NEITHER DO YOU TELL HIM ANYTHING THAT IS SAID IN THE COURSE OF BEING WITH AN INFORMANT FOR THE PURPOSE OF THE INTERVIEW. NO OTHER INFORMANT MUST KNOW WHO ELSE HAS BEEN SELECTED. (IN THIS RESPECT CONSIDER THE SIGNIFICANCE OF THE OFFICIAL SECRETS ACT, WHICH YOU HAVE SIGNED.)

(g) Your authorisation card and the schedules you are using on our behalf must be looked after carefully. If ever you lose any of these things **telephone us immediately**, never wait to see if they will turn up. Also advise the police in your area about the loss.

(h) You will normally have been told at a briefing if the subject matter of a survey is likely to result in pleas from the public for advice and whether in any circumstances you can offer any suggestions as to a department which they might consult. Unless you have been told at

the briefing that you can mention a source of advice you
cannot say or do anything, beyond stating that you are not
qualified to help them. Express your sorrow about this
and explain that we are a research unit only and know
little about particular social problems. If you are asked
for advice more than once then contact us about it. We
may be able to tell you how to avoid such queries.

(i) In the event of an accident occurring to you whilst on
duty, the accident should be reported immediately and
in writing to the Administration Officer.

Full details should be given of:

(i)   date and time of accident
(ii) place of accident
(iii) cause and nature of injury
(iv) time of starting and finishing work on day of accident.

In turn Field Branch need to know if the accident prevents
or disturbs your rate of work completion, particularly
if it means we need to find someone else to keep your
appointments at short notice.

(j) Always give us as much warning as possible if there is
a likelihood that you will need us to find someone else
to keep any future appointments for you on any survey.

(k) It is clear that to be an excellent interviewer you need
an all-round interest in the many subjects and the many
types of surveys we cover. It may happen that we carry
out one survey on a subject which is against your own
convictions. You have the right to refuse to work on such
an ad hoc survey but clearly we would not expect this to
happen more than once in an interviewer's lifetime, if
that frequently.

Much has been said about contacting headquarters whenever
you have problems related to your work. In general Field
Branch is the one with whom you will deal. On any specific
survey you will be told the research officer's telephone exten-
sion so that you can query direct with him specific instruction
about the subject matter of the survey. In turn you can telephone
Sampling Branch direct about any query address on your list.
For anything else, which means practically everything, contact
Field Branch. Which member of Field Branch you contact will
depend on your problem. Refer to your current list of which
members of staff handle allocating, work in progress and interviewing method to decide to whom you want to talk or write.

Mobile interviewers

When you are working away from your home base:

(i) **Call daily at Poste Restante G. P. O.** We will write you there whenever we have no other address for you. Once you have a temporary address let us have it. It may be quicker to contact you in an emergency at a temporary address rather than the G. P. O. where you call only once in 24 hours. Do remember on your last visit to the G. P. O. to ask them to re-direct any letters which may arrive after you have left the area.

(ii) **Complete work quickly whenever on subsistence**

    (a) In deciding what constitutes a reasonable day's work when on subsistence take into account that we expect a minimum 8-hour working day from you, of which no more than an hour should be travelling time. This means if you can find nowhere to stay in the immediate area in which you are to work, you will need to contact us to get authority to stay at a distance from it.

    (b) If your quota will take some two to three weeks to complete, whether one returns home to base weekends depends on whether the survey requires you to work Saturday or Friday evening and be back on duty Monday morning (as on occasion it does) and/or whether the cost of the fare home, plus travelling time, is more expensive than subsistence over the weekend. Treasury rulings on the number of nights one can stay in an area on subsistence are revised from time to time and you must make sure you know all the current rules governing subsistence before going away on it.

Chapter 15

GLOSSARY

It is necessary for us to have standardised operations to which clear and distinct names are given. In order that you can carry out these technical operations you must learn a little of the language of social research. Words that you will hear most often in the Government Social Survey occur in this chapter.

The following terms should not be inflicted on the public. They are our jargon and if used on the public will either be:

(a) unintelligible to them and make them regard you as a remote and stuffy individual.

(b) misunderstood, since the word's usual connotations may be at variance with its technical function.

BIAS	(interviewer's deadly sin) exerting any kind of influence which changes informants' natural response.
CLOSED (question)	one which defines its limits and prescribes terms in which we want informants to respond.
CODING	part of the process of analysing data obtained; by putting responses with arbitrary meanings into sets and alloting to each a figure or letter for brevity and purposes of addition.

159

CONURBA-TION	continuously built-up areas surrounding large population centres. Seven conurbations, e.g. Birmingham, Manchester, each dominated by major city which has grown steadily, absorbing smaller communities in its path.
DUMMY	a practice or trial interview to familiarise interviewer with schedule or quota and method of presentation. Used in a briefing as a means of explaining content of interview, or on a stranger to enable you to become au fait with layout before starting real quota.
FIELD	habitat or venue for interviewing. The process away from H.Q. covering your work, the public, and the places where you visit them.
FREE (interview)	Qualitative rather than quantitative interview. Used at pre-pilot stage to establish areas of interest within forthcoming survey. There are no set questions because it is exploratory and allows informant some freedom of choice on topics. Interviewer employs non-directional probes extensively to get topics covered in depth. Whole interview is recorded verbatim.
HEREDITA-MENT	an address, or parts of an address rated as separate units in the Rating Lists held by Local Authority areas.
INFORMANT	The person whom you interview. Occasionally referred to on schedule as "sjt" (subject) and in some organisations as interviewee.
LEAD	directing someone to answer in a specific way: prompting a desired answer and possibly inducing informant to reach a conclusion which may not reflect a true expression of his opinion or knowledge. This form of questioning would introduce bias when carried out by interviewer unbeknownst to research officer.

NEGATIVE questions

a form of leading question, e.g.

positive lead: *"you do like strawberries?"*

negative lead: *"you do not like strawberries do you?"*

where you put the idea of "not liking" into an informant's head he is most likely to agree rather than disagree with you, so from this form of question we can be no more certain of arriving at the truth than from a positive lead or suggestion to effect *"you do like strawberries?"*

NON-RESPONSE

generic term used to cover any of the given sample who you do not succeed in interviewing. The people we do not contact are a constant worry to us since the representativeness of our sample is diminished by the loss of any person. You have to supply precise data on reason for non-response; be it

(a) **refusal** by informant or on his behalf (and for what reason)

(b) **removal** of sampled person from address and/or **demolition** of a sampled premise.

(c) no contact possible; informant away for whole of sampling period (together with reason for absence).

NON-DIREC-TIONAL

a term often used in conjunction with the word **probe**, meaning use of an innocuous question which, by not directing the informant to one avenue of response, allows him freedom to respond in (almost) any fashion he choses.

of a question .....

one not pointing out conclusions but letting people choose and reach their own ...
one not indicating a point to which you want informant to move yet which urges him to move somewhere of his choosing.

OPEN (question)	See non-directional above. A question which conveys neither positive nor negative opinion on a topic.
examples of open question	*"Do you like any fruits or not?"*
and if yes	*"which fruits do you like?"*(unspecified) and record all given.
	(now look back to "lead" and "negatives" for wrong way to question)

PILOT	tryout of survey to decide form it should take; length of interview and types of questions. There can be many stages of piloting from initial group discussions and free interviews through semi to a wholly structured interview. An attempt to recreate in miniature the problems we may meet on main survey and thereby eliminate them before main field work is carried out.

PROBE	to explore, examine closely and encourage amplifications of response from informants.

PRECHECK	any immediate look through schedules as they come in from field. Usually two: one by Field Branch, for completeness, one by Coding Branch for individual question coding and unexplained inconsistencies.

PRECODES	suffix of a letter or figure recorded on schedule beside a defined category of response. They are usually given in a set to lessen the amount of writing you have to do during the interview. You ring appropriate suffix whenever that response is given. Precodes can be decided on whenever all divisions of responses are known in advance, e.g. informant is male (code) 1, female (code) 2.

162

PROMPT	assisting, by suggestion, sometimes used to curtail or channel informant's response. Prompting is carried out on research officer instruction only.
QUOTA	Your share of the total sample set for a survey. (Not to be confused with the term "quota" sample which is a type of sample less exact than "random" and not used in the Government Social Survey, other than on some pilots.)
RANDOM	The technical term for the type of representative sample used in the Government Social Survey . . . . . where a whole population is counted and all its members have an equal chance of being picked for interview.
ROLE	the part you play as interviewer with the person selected for interview ... to whom you give the role of informant.
SAMPLING	a method used to draw conclusions or gain information about the whole of a population by taking only a part of that group. This group or part of the whole population should be representative, so that its attributes and characteristics can be taken to indicate those of the whole population being studied.
SCHEDULE	document bearing questions to be asked of the informant and space to record the responses.
SIBLING	children of same parents. May be used to cover both brothers and sisters.
STRUC-TURED	an interview where terms to be used are defined. The order and form of the questions have been thought out so that the data collected can be added together because it results from the same form of questioning being used for all informants.

PAGE NUMBER REFERENCE ON TYPES OF QUESTION

Printed in England for Her Majesty's Stationery Office by
Hobbs the Printers Ltd., Millbrook, Southampton.
Dd 151501 K8 2/69 G3313